CHRISTIAN
WORSHIP

CHRISTIAN WORSHIP

Glorifying and Enjoying God

Ronald P. Byars

Foundations of Christian Faith
Published by Geneva Press in Conjunction with
the Office of Theology and Worship, Presbyterian Church (U.S.A.)

Book design by Sharon Adams
Cover design by Night & Day Design

First edition

Published by Geneva Press
Louisville, Kentucky

This book is printed on acid-free paper that meets the American National Standards Institute Z39.48 standard.

PRINTED IN THE UNITED STATES OF AMERICA

00 01 02 03 04 05 06 07 08 09 — 10 9 8 7 6 5 4 3 2 1

Library of Congress Cataloging-in-Publication Data is on file at the Library of Congress, Washington, D.C.

ISBN 0-664-50136-2

*For my companion at the table and at
the Holy Table,
Susan Rhodes Byars*

Contents

Series Foreword

*T*he books in the Foundations of Christian Faith series explore central elements of Christian belief. These books are intended for persons on the edge of faith as well as for those with strong Christian commitment. The writers are women and men of vital faith and keen intellect who know what it means to be an everyday Christian.

Each of the twelve books in the series focuses on a theme central to the Christian faith. The authors hope to encourage you as you grapple with the big, important issues that accompany our faith in God. Thus, Foundations of Christian Faith includes volumes on the Trinity, what it means to be human, worship and sacraments, Jesus Christ, the Bible, the Holy Spirit, the church, life as a Christian, political and social engagement, religious pluralism, creation and new creation, and dealing with suffering.

You may read one or two of the books that deal with issues you find particularly interesting, or you may wish to read them all in order to gain a deeper understanding of your faith. You may read the books by yourself or together with others. In any event, I trust that you will find a fuller awareness of the living God who is made known in Jesus Christ through the present power of the Holy Spirit. Christian faith is not about the mastery of ideas. It is about encountering the living God. It is my confident hope that this series of books will lead you more deeply into that encounter.

Charles Wiley
Office of Theology and Worship
Presbyterian Church (U.S.A.)

1

What's the Point?

Why Do People Worship?

On Fridays, Muslims in Dearborn, Michigan, and Lexington, Kentucky, gather for worship, much as they do in Teheran, Riyadh, or Ramallah. They chant prayers in the Arabic language as the men (in front) and the women (behind) alternately bow their foreheads to the ground and then rise. In Delhi or Calcutta, devout Hindus make their way to their favorite temple, where they make a small offering to Krishna or Lakshmi. After sunset on the same Friday, lights shine from the windows of temples and synagogues in Long Island or Tiberias or Lincoln, Nebraska, as Jews gather for prayer. Late Saturday afternoon, cars begin to fill the parking lot at St. Mary's in Lompoc, discharging passengers headed for the vigil mass. On Sunday morning, the Presbyterians in Charlotte and the Methodists in Nashville and the Lutherans in St. Paul collect themselves for church.

Can't these folks think of something better to do? There is always business to tend to. There are chores to be done, books to read, movies to see, games to watch, web sites to surf. What motivates people to abandon the television and postpone a visit to the mall in order to worship? There is no one-size-fits-all answer. Some worship to meet somebody else's expectations. Some worship out of pure habit. Some worship in spite of—or because of—the fact that they are locked in some kind of struggle with God, whom they experience as an adversary. But many feel themselves drawn to worship—though they may not be able to say why. Some vital instinct rises up to praise the One from whom our lives—and all lives—have sprung. The majesty of the Divine evokes praise, much as a spectacular sunset moves even the atheist to a sense of awe. A deeply rooted human impulse urges us to bless the Power that formed the universe and keeps it in motion. People worship because it comes as naturally as eating and drinking. We simply can't help it.

What Distinguishes Worship from Other Human Activities?

In centuries past—and still today in many parts of the world—worship flowed naturally from the deepest human impulses. However, the complexity of modern society may have scrambled those impulses. The twentieth century marks a significant cultural turning point. The emergence of electronic media—particularly television and the computer—has introduced ways of perceiving, thinking, and relating to the world in strikingly new ways. Just as the invention of the printing press changed the way people understood their own lives, the electronic media have overturned the old order. One result is that many contemporary people have become estranged from their inner selves. What once was natural now seems distant, inaccessible. To North American people at the dawn of the twenty-first century, worship may seem odd indeed. In most places and times, parents and societies communicated to their children a sense of the holy. From childhood on, one learned to understand the meaning of life in terms of one's relations with other people and whatever divine powers there might be. We may be inclined to scorn the ancient ways as unsophisticated—even superstitious. And yet stories told around the fireplace or the common table introduced the very young to the fact that they belonged to something bigger than self or family or tribe. From that sense of a larger belonging there sprang a sense of awe—of indebtedness, perhaps—even gratitude.

We socialize young children in our society, too. We have schools, churches, synagogues, Brownies, Cub Scouts, soccer leagues—and television. Which, do you suppose, makes the largest impact? According to some accounts, a child will have absorbed 30,000 television ads before entering first grade. Adolescents will spend more time with advertisements than the entire length of their academic experience in high school. In comparison, 52 hours of religious education a year are pitifully few. Which way of viewing the world and one's place in it is likely to prevail?

For all practical purposes, television produces entertainment as a means of getting people to watch commercials. Whatever the content of television shows themselves, the commercials communicate a philosophy of life. Of course, they don't announce that they are proclaiming a philosophy of life. Nevertheless, the constantly reiterated message of commercials is that the purpose of life is to make money and buy things. The suggestion that we belong to anything or anyone larger than ourselves is hard to find on any channel. The tragic sense of life that overtakes so many has to be worked into an hour-long time slot, if it appears at all. Sentimentality rules, and the big questions surface only briefly in documentaries or the rare, challenging drama. Why are we on the planet? It would seem that we inhabit the earth in order to play volleyball on the beach, drink Coca-Cola, dazzle people with our smiles, and beat out the competition. The commercial constantly drums these messages and others like them into the ears of the tiniest persons seated or sprawled in front of the television set. The message is powerful and nearly inescapable. Compared to the resources available to the commercial culture, even the best of formal religious education programs are likely to be completely drowned out.

We are socializing our children into a small universe with small purposes. Technology awes us with each new product, but the awe doesn't last. The schools teach us about the age of the universe and subatomic physics, but that universe feels like a lonely place. The possibility has been ruled out that beyond it all there is a Reality before Which (or Whom) we must cry "Holy!" The contemporary world leaves little room for taking such a possibility seriously. How can it, if the point of life is to get money and buy stuff?

Those Who Worship
Inhabit a Bigger Universe

People of Christian faith suspect that hidden deep within every human being is a need to praise the Life that made us and sustains us. At least, that suspicion has been borne out in the experience of Christian people. We have praised God because it is our duty, but also because it is our delight. In the praise of God we have poured out our hearts and, often quite by surprise, find that the Spirit has filled them again. And yet the praise we rightly owe to God has often failed to find its target. Human beings frequently misdirect their reverence. We find ourselves in awe of something God has made rather than in awe of God. Longing to find the levers that control things, people have tried to domesticate God. We know how to give our hearts away, but frequently we give them to what the Bible has called idols. Worship focused on the BIG God of the biblical story doesn't always square with pledges promiscuously given to lesser objects of allegiance. A pervasive secularism has not smothered every impulse to worship. However, it has scattered that impulse, disguised it, and often hidden it even from the one who feels it without being able to identify it. Some who would never describe themselves as religious are moved nevertheless to find Something (Someone?) to give themselves to.

The weekly assembly for Christian worship may seem strange—even incomprehensible—to those socialized to relate first of all to the small screen of television or computer. If the purpose of our lives is to mimic the way characters in commercials live, worship may quite likely seem boring. Worship challenges life conformed to the dimensions of the small screen. Or, in reverse, the life of the small screen challenges life as conceived in worship. In contrast with life as viewed through a 36-inch screen, worship seems an odd affair indeed. Prostrating oneself—or simply bowing one's head—seems at odds with the project of building one's self-esteem. Elegant language with scriptural rhythms seems out of sync to ears tuned to the meter of commercials. Solemn rituals using bread and wine puzzle folks who seldom pause for a meal with the whole household. What is this extravagant language of praise? If there is some Force that governs the whole universe, does it (he? she?) need to be flattered? The assembly gathered for worship finds itself drawn into a larger universe than the universe in which the point is to get money and buy stuff. The intention of Christian worship is to develop what someone has called "imaginative vision." That vision enables us to see the world as one might see it looking through God's eyes—not as the world ordinarily presents itself, but as God intends it to be.

At worship, we trace our origins to some stirring even before the Big Bang that launched the universe. At worship, we find ourselves oriented to an ultimate future that beckons us homeward even though moon, sun, solar system, galaxy—the universe itself—be reduced to darkness. At worship, our consciousness becomes alert to the possibility that there may be One who, as the old spiritual puts it, "holds the whole world" in capable hands. Here lies the strangeness of worship. In worship, we gather in the presence of One who was before us; who will be after we are gone; and who, despite our smallness and the brevity of our lives, invites us to some kind of relationship. To see our lives against such a vastness—yet with the possibility of intimacy at its heart—seems altogether different from the notion that the real world has been captured in the raptures of the beautiful and contented people in the ads. Who, do you suppose, has got it right?

Some Characteristics of Christian Worship

In the assembly for Christian worship, we step into a larger reality than the one that occupies us most of the time. At worship, we meet an invitation to act on our impulse to offer praise and thanks for gifts not of our own making—whether or not we recognized that impulse. When we fail to recognize it, the impulse is nevertheless at work in us, creating a restlessness we cannot name. But in those who sense the reality of the holy, there rises up a sense of awe.

Other religious communities worship in ways very specific to their own sense of identity. Some religions worship more than one god—often associating each with some force in the natural world or in human nature. Some, like traditional Buddhists, would not speak of a God or gods at all. In other cases, although the word God is used, it has very different associations than it has in another religious tradition. How might we distinguish specifically Christian worship from other kinds of worship?

Christian worship celebrates Christ's victory over death and evil through his crucifixion and resurrection. Christians offer their worship to God in Christ's name, through the Holy Spirit. Christian worship is and must be an engagement not with some generic god, but with precisely this God—revealed as Father, Son, and Holy Spirit. The shorthand way Christians use to speak of the God they worship is Holy Trinity. When Christians speak of the God of whom the Bible testifies, they speak of a God who is three-in-one. Often, people raised in Christian churches and exposed to Christian worship for decades are surprised to hear that the Holy Trinity is any more than a doctrinal sideshow. The truth is that the three-in-one rests as the very foundation of our faith and our worship. It may be that we Christians have obscured the fact that our worship is, first of all, Trinitarian. Are we embarrassed, perhaps, by the doctrine of the Trinity? Maybe it's too puzzling. It might be too hard to explain. Or possibly we, the worshipers, simply have become so accustomed to certain kinds of language that we don't really hear it any more.

In the Yellow Pages of most phone books issued in larger communities, you can find all sorts of church bodies, including Baptist, United Methodist, and Unitarian-Universalist congregations. The name Unitarian reminds us of a dispute that broke apart the Congregational churches of New England in the 1700s. The word suggests that it came into being to counter the word Trinitarian. One cannot easily characterize contemporary Unitarians. The first Unitarians were those who could not understand or accept Christian faith in God as three-in-one—Holy Trinity. Unitarians share with Muslims and others the suspicion that when Christians speak of the Trinity, it's merely a disguised way of speaking of what are, in fact, three gods. There seems to be no compromise. Certainly it must be that there is one God—or perhaps three—but not both.

Christian Worship is Trinitarian

It's easy to sympathize with the problem critics have with the Trinity. The mathematics simply don't work out. We sensed the problem even before skeptics pointed it out to us. That may be why we have been so reluctant to speak of God as Trinity. And yet, we must. The doctrine of the Trinity is not some add-on option at the margins of our faith. Rather, it lies at its very center. The doctrine of the Trinity defines God as God is known in the Christian church.

This doctrine was not simply dreamed up by folks lodged in some ivory tower. It's not the result of some mad philosopher in love with the idea of making the simple into something complex. The doctrine of the Trinity doesn't trace its origins to some library, or a seminar, or to a hermit driven to distraction by the need to describe God. The doctrine of the Trinity is rooted, first and foremost, in the experience of the Christian community. It begins with the first Christians' encounter with Jesus Christ.

The early Christians, like their Jewish forebears, were already acquainted with the God whose power created something out of nothing. They prayed as Jews prayed, with faces raised toward heaven, hands extended upward, toward the God who is above everything that exists. This God, whose name devout Jews had been forbidden to speak aloud, stirred them to silence, and awakened their awe. Later generations built churches whose lines led the eye upward, reminding of the God who is above all and over all.

Yet the early Christian community faced a real dilemma when they tried to say who Jesus Christ is. They had become acquainted with Jesus of Nazareth, a Jewish carpenter who enjoyed a good meal, wept real tears, and bled when he was injured. There was no question that he was human, just like the rest of us. But, that's not all he was. Wherever he went, he altered things in the immediate environment. With a word or a touch, he set down God's healing rule in the midst of those who were broken, sick, alienated, despised, rebellious, arrogant.

Those who witnessed the powerful effect of Jesus' ministry handed on their testimony of the work he had done among them. He fed the multitudes—set a table before them "in the presence of their enemies." He calmed storms within and without. He restored people to their right minds. He confronted those who used power in petty or cruel ways. He called forth life out of the places of the dead. In his crucifixion, he embraced human cruelty and vengefulness without passing it on—meeting viciousness with redeeming love. In his resurrection, God claimed the last Word—and it was a Word of a love more powerful than death.

To sum up, Jesus brought God's ultimate future—where God's reign shall have come and God's will shall be done—and set it among the people as a down payment on what is yet to come. Whoever had eyes to see could catch a glimpse in the present moment of what God is preparing for us in God's own good time. Who was this person?

The community of Christian believers had to speak the truth they'd learned in their own experience as a people. Though they'd met in Jesus of Nazareth a human being like the rest of us, this Jesus was also the bearer of God's very person and presence. Could they—can we?—explain how God can bend down and enter our experience from the inside—born of a woman, just as we are? There is no way to explain it because there are no precedents. Nevertheless, the Christian community has been compelled to testify to what it has seen and heard. What it has seen and heard is that the God who is *up there*, so to speak—has also come to walk *beside* us.

The earliest Christian communities would not have been honest to their own experience had they not spoken of God both as *above* and *alongside*. But those encounters didn't exhaust their experience of God. The community gathered around the risen Lord also had had experience of God within them and among them. Upon hearing of Jesus Christ, crucified and risen, something inside them had shifted. Something deep within had come to life; had risen up to take hold of what was offered. They discovered in themselves the gift of faith. Whatever force had been at work inside them to kindle faith had also brought them close to others who had had the same experience. They had found themselves drawn into a community—a community of faith, a community of the resurrection. They became a part of a people—or, as one early leader put it, the household of God.

During his ministry, Jesus had promised that when he was no longer physically present among the disciples, there would be given a Holy Spirit. The first Christians experienced this very Spirit at work in them and among them. They knew the Spirit not as an independent spiritual force, or as another deity. The Holy Spirit led them to Jesus Christ, and through him, to the Father. They identified this Holy Spirit as nothing less than the God they had already met as one above and alongside them. The Spirit had been at work in their hearts, raising faith and forging them into a community. They knew that there was only one God. They also knew that they could not possibly speak adequately of this God if they did not speak of the God *above*, the God *alongside*, and the God *within-and-among* them. Not three Gods, mind you, but one. God had risked revealing God's three-in-oneness to us despite our impatience with mystery. Borrowing the language Jesus had used, they spoke of this one God as Father, Son, and Holy Spirit.

This way of experiencing God and speaking about God isn't the product of common-sense reasoning. To conceive of God as one-in-three, three-in-one, is certainly strange even from the point of view of most of the religious people in the world. And yet we believe that it tells the truth about God—truth that would remain forever hidden from human beings had God not chosen to reveal it.

No comparison can be pushed too far, but perhaps there is something in our own experience that may offer some insight. I am—at one and the same time—somebody's son, somebody's husband, and somebody's father. I present myself to my parents in certain well-accustomed ways that lie deep within my identity as their child. With my wife, I draw from different reservoirs of my inner being. When I'm with my children, the parental part of me comes to the fore. My parents know that I am a husband and a father as well as their son. My wife knows that I am a son and a parent as well as her spouse. My children are well aware of the other dimensions of who I am. I never stop being son, spouse, and father—all at once, yet without compromising the fact that I am one unified person. Within myself, I am in fact what I present to each. Similarly, the God who walks *alongside* us is always at the same time also the God who is at work *in and among* us, without ever ceasing to be the God who is high *above* all things.

It is the one God, the true and only God, who has graciously revealed God's inner life to us. And it is this inner life of God that shapes Christian worship—to the Father, through Christ, empowered and lifted by the Holy Spirit.

Does God Have Gender?

Ah, but there are protests. Holy Spirit may be all right. But what is this business of *Father* and *Son*? We live, after all, in an age enlightened about gender equality. Are we supposed to presume that God is male? The answer is decisively No. In fact, the Bible (remarkably for its origins in a male-oriented culture) sometimes uses images in reference to God that most of us would take as feminine. It may speak of God as a mother, who bends down to watch over and shelter her children; as a woman searching for a lost coin; and even as a nursing mother. The point of the Father-Son language is not to identify God as male. Of course, God is beyond all gender. The Father-Son language borrows intimate and personal ways of speaking in preference to abstract and impersonal ways. The Christian church has not experienced God as an It, nor merely as some kind of force. We can only speak of the God we have known if we use the language of the family. The use of Father-Son language is not meant to make special claims for the male half of the human race, nor to exclude the female half.

Unfortunately, we have not been successful in identifying gender-neutral language that retains the intimacy of family relationships. Until we do, the church continues to use these familiar terms, learned in its infancy, from scripture. Though we may supplement Father, Son, and Holy Spirit with other ways of referring to God, this triune name is not dispensable because they are relational terms, rooted in scripture. Scripture has a special authority in the church. That authority rests in the fact that scripture summarizes the heart and soul of the Christian faith—that which we learned from the Hebrews as well as that which we learned at the feet of Jesus and in the early congregations gathered around the risen Lord. And so we do not discard the ancient names— Father, Son, Holy Spirit. And yet we yearn for ways to testify to our conviction that God is like a mother and sister as well as like a father and brother.

Pulled In and Sent Out

Christian worship may be distinguished from other kinds of worship in that those who are pulled in are also sent out. We come to praise and thank God, to listen for a Word from God, and to draw strength from God. But the church exists for the sake of the world. In ancient times, the Hebrew people understood themselves to be God's chosen people. Although chosenness has often been misunderstood—even in Biblical times—it is not a sign of special privilege. God chose Israel for special service. That chosenness is both delight and burden. When God called Abraham, and promised that he and Sarah would become the ancestors of a multitude of people, God declared the purpose of this choosing: "In you all the families of the earth shall be blessed" (Gen. 12:3b). In other words, God chose Israel not to set Israel above other peoples, but to be a blessing to them all. Similarly, Jesus chose disciples, saying, "You did not choose me, but I chose you . . ." (John 15:16). The church of Jesus Christ shares in Israel's mission to be a blessing to all the families of the earth. It doesn't exist only for its own sake, but as those who bear the burden—and experience the delight—of being God's witness in the world—a servant people. In a letter to an early church, an apostle put it like this: "You are a chosen race, a royal priesthood, a holy nation, God's own people, in order that you may proclaim the mighty acts of him who called you out of darkness into his marvelous light" (1 Pet. 2:9).

The church's worship is distinctive in that it is like inhaling and exhaling. There is a rhythm of assembling, then scattering. We gather around baptismal font, pulpit, and table to be washed, fortified, and nourished for our return to the world. As each service reaches its conclusion, the assembled congregation receives a blessing. We go out as those whom Jesus Christ has commissioned to be his servants wherever our lives and work take us.

Another distinction of Christian worship is that, no matter how threatening the day, worship always takes place in a framework of hope. Hope is not the same as wishful thinking. The congregation expresses its distinctive Christian hope when it prays, "Thy kingdom come; Thy will be done on earth as it is in heaven." Jesus' ministry was a promise—in words and in action—that God's will would in fact be done. Though we live in a world that seems at times to be reeling out of control, God is still steering the ship, and will bring it safely to port. Daily, the newscasts report incidents of outrageous unfairness. The natural world produces earthquakes, wind, fire, and flood—each claiming its share of victims. Human beings turn on each other in hair-raising acts of callousness and brutality. Some have too much and others have too little. The innocent suffer and the guilty flourish. The powerful have little regard for those who have no power. In short, though life is a gift and the world may be a delight, it is not what we sense it ought to be.

The whole thrust of Jesus' presence and activity among us was to say that God hasn't finished with the world yet. The day of God's joyful triumph will come, and when it does, the uneven places will be evened out. Jesus spoke of the kingdom of heaven. Some prefer to speak of the reign of God. Whatever words we choose, the point is that God intends to have the last word, and that it will be a good word. We need not worry unduly about outcomes, because God is in charge of that department.

In the meantime, those who have caught a glimpse of what God's reign will be like have a job to do. Not only are we to pray for the coming of God's kingdom, but we are also to do our best to reshape the bent and broken places in this world, wherever we are able. All Christian worship leans into God's coming reign, inviting trust in the One who will make all things new.

Hope is not complacency. Hope is not indifferent to the hurts and wrongs of this present age, as though God's promised kingdom absolves us of all responsibility. We live toward hope, but we are also bearers of hope. It is not possible to turn our backs on the world. We may not be silent where we see wrongs. We may not refuse to love the world: "For God so loved the world that he gave his only Son . . ." (John 3:16a). One of the reasons for worshiping is that in worship, God picks us up, brushes us off, and replenishes our store of love—for God, and for God's world. Hope, then, is not dreamy-eyed. It's not a sort of anaesthetic that numbs our ability to feel the pain that's present in this life. Hope is active and expectant. Hope equips us to do what we have to do.

Christian Worship
Pulls Us Out of Isolation

In some religious communities, an assembly for worship is rare. The normal way of worshiping is one at a time. The worshiper goes to the temple when she or he feels like it, and offers a gift or prays all alone. In other religious communities, such as Judaism, private worship only supplements the public worship of an assembled congregation. These communities understand themselves to be bound together as a people. For Christianity in particular, worship is distinguished by the fact that it is the offering of a people linked together in covenant with Jesus Christ and one another. The doctrine of the Trinity shows us that in the very heart of God, there is community—the Father with the Son, the Son with the Holy Spirit, the Holy Spirit with the Father, etc. A famous icon by the Russian artist Rublev depicts the three "persons" of the Trinity in intimate communion with one another. Under the guise of the three angels who visited Abraham, they sit in a close circle. Rublev intends for us to see that at the very heart of God there is relationship. For Christians, there is no such thing as an authentic faith that is limited to "God and Me" or "Me and Jesus." Those who have to do with God must also have to do with one another.

Twentieth-century American Protestants are likely not to know this, or to have forgotten it. Our society tends to see the world as an enormous cafeteria of choices. Someone who more or less believes the Christian faith may or may not choose to go to church. There are folks who identify themselves as Christians who nevertheless consider worship an occasional exercise, of which we avail ourselves in times of special need, or when the mood strikes us. Or, who worship quite regularly and nevertheless see worship as something offered to those who come primarily to consume something: learning, inspiration, ethical direction, an aesthetic experience, etc. If one needs none of those things at the moment, public worship is unnecessary, so the reasoning goes. For others, worship is almost exclusively private, having nothing to do with anyone else.

These views, though widely held, are vast misconceptions. The New Testament has absolutely no knowledge of any sort of Christian faith that's purely private, separated from the community of faith. By Biblical definitions, to be a Christian is by its very nature to be incorporated into a body—the "body of Christ." Apart from that body, there are no Christians—whatever a person's private belief system. Those who are unable to meet with the community due to illness or disability are nevertheless bound to it by prayer and sacrament. Our gracious God may very well heal and save people outside the Christian church—who are we to say?—but one cannot be a Christian apart from the people of God. Christian worship, rightly conceived, is an exercise of the body of Christ. However scrupulously we may practice disciplines of private devotion, they are no substitutes for the church's assembly for worship in common. We are organically connected to the body. A Christian spiritual life both sustains the body of Christ and is sustained by it. Worship is both duty and delight, for it is in worship that the people who together make up Christ's body on earth have engaged to meet the risen Lord.

So, what makes Christian worship distinct from other sorts of worship? It is Trinitarian. The Christian assembly always meets with an eye to the horizon, in expectation of the coming of the reign of God—God's peaceable kingdom. Christian worship is rooted in hope—confident that God will heal the whole creation and us with it, exactly as promised. Christian worship is a rhythm of being gathered and being sent. And Christian worship is not merely a gathering of like-minded individuals who have more or less the same opinions about matters of faith. It is, rather, an organically related body, each member necessary to the whole.

That Doesn't Sound Like Our Church

Worship as we experience it may seem quite different from these rather grand descriptions of it. It's hard to think of us as bound together in one body when there are so many of us who are grateful that we see each other only once a week. In the pew across the aisle there's a man who's been married and divorced four times. The usher who led us to our seat works for a realtor who's rumored to steer African-American buyers away from mostly white neighborhoods. In this community of hope, we sit behind a woman so pessimistic that she doesn't renew her magazine subscriptions until the very last minute, for fear she'll die before she gets the first one. Are we Trinitarian? A young woman in the choir has carefully explained to her daughter that since God is love, Love must be God. In the congregation is a man who complains that every time he comes to church, they sing the same two hymns. It's either *Silent Night* or *Jesus Christ Is Risen Today*. A few speak of paying their dues, as though they belong to an organization that promises certain privileges in exchange for money. One of these begrudges every nickel sent to support causes beyond the local congregation.

Studies have sometimes shown that the attitudes and viewpoints of people who go to church are scarcely any different from those of people who don't go to church. So, how is it possible to claim that worship makes a difference? If it really mattered, it would seem as though the pews would be filled with people all of whom are hopeful, generous, outward-looking, reverent in unassuming ways, and clearly able to explain the Christian faith. If it really made a difference, the church would be an assembly of those who have already been healed and made whole—clear examples of virtue and integrity. If worship really is as powerful as claimed, services would be filled with people known to their neighbors as models of how human beings ought to be. But it doesn't always work out that way, does it?

In the first congregation I served, one of the committees organized teams of people to call on unchurched persons in the community who might conceivably be prospective members. Jesse Davis—an elder of the church in every beautiful way associated with the word—went to call on a man who may have entered the church doors one time a decade earlier. The fellow said to Jesse, "I'm not going to that church. It's full of hypocrites." Jesse replied, "There's always room for one more."

The church doesn't set out to be hypocritical, or consider hypocrisy a matter of indifference. However, wherever human beings gather—and for whatever purpose—hypocrisy gathers with them, along with the whole multitude of human sins and failings. If the church were only for the perfected and the virtuous, where would the sinners go? Where would the wounded find any refuge? Where would the broken go for healing? It's become a commonplace to say that the church is not a museum of saints, but a hospital for sinners. It is, in fact, a mixed gathering of people who are both virtuous and compromised, strong and weak, rejoicing and lamenting, recovering from our wounds, and perhaps close to despairing of any hope of recovery. It takes all these and more to make a worshiping community. If we speak about worship in rather grand terms, it is because there is in fact something great at work in these assemblies of quite ordinary, quite predictable people. There is, in fact, an amazing grace there, doing its quiet but remarkable work. The source of that amazing grace, Christians believe, is none other than the God-who-is-for-us: Father, Son, and Holy Spirit. This God is the fountain of all the goodness there is. This God is at work in our gathered life to heal, confront, strengthen, warn, encourage, console, instruct, and raise life even where all evidence of life has fled.

Can we measure God's work among us with some kind of electronic measuring device? By taking a survey? Or recording the observations of neutral parties? Of course not. But it remains the testimony of generations of Christian people that in worship they have met God and become engaged with God. Are their lives better than the lives of their nonparticipating neighbors? A better question might be, "How do their lives compare with what they might have been apart from this community of faith and worship?"

Christian worship both resembles and is distinguished from the worship of other religious communities. It shares with those other communities the fact that it is always very human beings who engage in worship—the same human beings who eat, sleep, procreate, govern and are governed, argue, fight, invent, build and tear down, deface beauty and create it. It is different from those other communities in that it is first of all a community gathered around the person of Jesus Christ. Not just the *idea* of someone *like* Jesus Christ—but Jesus Christ in particular. Without him we may be religious, but we are not Christian. We may be virtuous, moral, and upright—but without him, we are not Christian. We may be spiritual—but if we have not gathered around him, we are not Christian. Christian worship is Christian exactly because it is rooted in the same Jesus Christ who declared, "You did not choose me, but I chose you. . . ."

2

The Shape of Christian Worship

It's Not All the Same!

*I*f you drive south on I-75 from Detroit to Cincinnati, you will see several enormous buildings that obviously house Christian congregations of some kind. None of these bear denominational names. State-of-the-art electronic signs flash a message or an invitation along with the name of the group that meets there. They may be called something like World Harvest Worship Center, or Solid Rock Church. These are independent Christian congregations. To varying degrees, these churches and their leadership pride themselves on having broken with tradition. If you were to visit one of these churches on Sunday morning—or Saturday evening—it's hard to say exactly what sort of worship you might find there. Sometimes it may resemble an old-fashioned revival meeting, electronically updated. At other times, worship may feel a lot more like entertainment. The building itself may have the atmosphere of a mall, a bank—or a living room. It may not seem at all like the kind of place we usually think of when we think of church.

Away from the interstate—closer to the center of town—those passing through will be more likely to see churchy churches: neo-Gothic, neocolonial, or what we have learned to call modern. Sometimes it's hard to find any sign identifying what these churches are. If there is a sign, it may be hard to read, with lettering too small, facing the street in such a way as to appeal to pedestrians, but unreadable to those driving by. These are traditional churches—Episcopal, Presbyterian, Catholic, Methodist, Lutheran. If you should arrive in time for worship, you may encounter a variety of styles and formats. Still, it's likely that the order of service will be somewhat predictable. The congregation will sing hymns; there will be prayers; someone will read scripture and preach a sermon. In certain churches, a minister will preside at the Eucharist, or Lord's Supper—if not every week, then at stated intervals. Sometimes there will be a baptism.

Who says what worship ought to be like? Who says what's essential for worship? Who says what's essential architecturally? Who says whether worship should be modeled after a pep rally, a concert, a motivational seminar, or a classroom exercise? All of the above? Or none of the above? By what authority does anyone decide what's appropriate for Christian worship and what's not?

Tradition vs. Traditionalism

We live in a society that's deeply suspicious of tradition. If we were to pick one word most often used in advertising, it might very well be *new*. New is always preferable to the old in a society whose tradition is to scorn tradition. And yet there is simply no human endeavor that has no connections with the ways things have been done before. The church organized specifically to reach out to seekers (persons outside the church who may be open to a spiritual quest) breaks with churchly tradition, but it does not hesitate to make use of secular traditions. For example, the worship place may look like a mall, feel like a theater. The traditions of the mall and of the spectacle may seem as up-to-date as today's breakfast rolls, but they are still traditions. A tradition is something that has been handed on. The antitradition church nevertheless hands on a tradition, though it may be one created in a secular, commercial environment. The twentieth-century American mall hands on a tradition rooted in the earlier department store and the still earlier public marketplace. The theater, even with its state-of-the-art electronics, hands on the feel and style of an ancient institution designed for entertainment. It is extremely unlikely that any contemporary institution can invent itself from scratch without any reference at all to some sort of tradition. The question is not whether tradition will influence us, but rather, *which* tradition will have the greatest impact?

It may be that our typically American distaste for tradition may stem, in fact, from unpleasant experiences with tradition*ism*. Tradition and traditionalism are not the same things. Tradition hands on from one generation to another those things found useful. Tradition doesn't attempt to suppress new experience or insight. Tradition is a treasury of experience from which we may draw for our benefit. Traditionalism, on the other hand, is rigid and exclusive, insisting on conformity even when no one any longer remembers what value a practice is meant to represent. Tradition is a gift of earlier generations. Traditionalism is narrow and oppressive—not a gift, but an imposition. People's negative associations with tradition may be based on their revulsion against traditionalism. Traditionalism gives tradition a bad name—unfairly, and unfortunately. Scorn for traditionalism may encourage indifference to precious things we might learn to value from tradition.

The truth is, of course, that churches have often been guilty of traditionalism. Someone has suggested that the seven last words of the church might be "We've never done it that way before!" It wouldn't be hard to find examples of churches that have invested too much in their traditions. Things that have been precious to one generation have been required of another for no apparent reason. But on the other hand, those whose disposition has been to despise tradition have often learned their scorn not from personal experience, but from forebears who passed on the habit. To reject tradition wholesale risks losing something of potentially enormous value. Do you suppose a better strategy might be to examine a particular tradition before rejecting it? Then, having become acquainted with it, to decide whether to value it, amend it, or discard it?

There is a body of tradition rooted in scripture. Things cherished by early generations have been handed on from age to age, taking root in a great variety of soils. They have endured in all sorts of cultures and circumstances. When they have been abused or neglected, they rise again to the surface in times that cry out for renewal.

Tradition Rooted in Scripture

The worship of the church stems from a tradition that has its roots in scripture, and in the communities from which our scriptures emerged. If one should ask, "Who says we should worship this way, or that way?" we might look first to scripture. Does scripture offer any useful models for Christian worship? Do those models, formed in an ancient culture, have any authority today? How has scripture shaped a tradition of Christian worship?

Imagine, if you can, a narrow street in Jerusalem, sometime near the middle of the first century. It's Saturday evening. The Sabbath officially ended at sunset. According to Jewish reckoning, the new day—Sunday—has already begun. At first one might see an individual here and there hurrying toward a doorway where they are quickly admitted. Then come others—in twos and threes, sometimes with children—perhaps carrying some sort of lantern to light the way. Their destination is an ordinary house in an ordinary neighborhood. There is nothing to indicate that the house is different from any other. Neighbors may know that the family who lives there are among those Jews who believe that Jesus is the Messiah. Their custom is to host the weekly gathering of believers in Jesus. What do they do there, in their modest assembly?

The first Christians were Jews. Jewish people had been worshiping God for many centuries. It should not be surprising to learn that Christian worship had been influenced by Jewish worship. At the very first, those who had come to believe that Jesus was the Messiah—the Christ—had continued to worship with other Jews. That meant keeping a special day set apart from other days of the week. That day was the Sabbath—Saturday, the seventh day. On the Sabbath it had become customary to assemble in the synagogue.

The synagogue, many believe, developed during the Babylonian exile—that period during which a triumphant Babylonian army had relocated much of the population of Jerusalem. The invaders had leveled the great Temple at Jerusalem, with its armies of priests and its many sacrificial rites. Taken to Babylon as captives, the exiles despaired, fearing that apart from the holy land, it would not be possible to worship God. Those exiles discovered, however, that the God of their forebears remained accessible even in the foreign place. The synagogues they created offered a quite different way of worship than that of the Temple rites. The synagogue in some ways resembled a school. There the devout studied the scriptures. There also, on the Sabbath, they sang hymns, prayed, and listened to scripture read and interpreted. It was synagogue worship that the first Christians knew best. In fact, Christians continued to worship in the synagogues until they were no longer welcome.

Those first Christians, however, required an assembly uniquely their own as well. On the first day of the week—Sunday, a working day—they found time to gather after having kept a holy Sabbath, according to Jewish custom. They might have gathered in the dusk that marked the beginning of the first day of the week— or maybe at first light, or possibly after finishing their work on Sunday. Sunday was not the Sabbath, which they continued to observe. They called Sunday by another name—the Lord's Day. Jesus had risen from the dead on the first day of the week. It was his resurrection that their Sunday assembly honored. This assembly was primarily for the purpose of eating and drinking what they called the Lord's Supper. It was, in fact, an actual meal—not entirely unlike today's church dinner—that reached its climax in the blessing and distribution of bread and wine.

Synagogue and Meal

After a time, traditional Jewish worshipers had become exasperated with those among them who believed in Jesus. The synagogues had pushed the Jewish Christians out as the two communities separated. No longer made to feel at home in the synagogue, the first Christians nevertheless valued the worship they had learned there. When they became a distinct community, assembling on Sunday, they began to combine the two forms of worship they had known. Early Christian worship united patterns inherited from the synagogue with patterns based on meals eaten with Jesus. A Sunday assembly for worship would begin with elements from the synagogue—scripture read and interpreted, prayers, hymns—and then move to the meal.

Worship in the earliest Christian congregations probably varied somewhat from place to place, and certainly over time. However, the New Testament gives us some clues about the sorts of things that were included in their services. In the letter to the Philippians, there is a poetic section that is understood to be an early Christian hymn. It praises Christ "who, though he was in the form of God, did not regard equality with God as something to be exploited, but emptied himself . . ." (Phil. 2:6–11). A section of the letter to the Ephesians that begins "Blessed be the God and Father of our Lord Jesus Christ, who has blessed us in Christ with every spiritual blessing in the heavenly places, etc." may very well also be a creed or other liturgical formula recited in worship. Ephesians 5:14 is likely a fragment of an early Christian hymn or chant sung at baptism: "Sleeper, awake! Rise from the dead and Christ will shine on you." Scholars estimate that various New Testament writings contain anywhere from five to thirty hymns. Scripture makes clear that there was some kind of offering—the collection of alms for the poor or those in special need. "On the first day of every week, each of you is to put aside and save whatever extra you earn . . ." (1 Cor. 16:2). Various persons had roles to play and gifts to offer in the worshiping assembly. The apostle Paul wrote, "When you come together, each one has a hymn, a lesson, a revelation, a tongue, or an interpretation" (1 Cor. 14:26). They offered prayer. A brief summary of early worship traditions appears in Acts 2:42: "They devoted themselves to the apostles' teaching and fellowship, to the breaking of bread and the prayers."

With all its variations, the basic pattern—combining synagogue worship with the Lord's Supper—developed early and persisted even when congregations became more and more to be made up of Gentiles (non-Jews). In this way Christian worship developed its unique shape, centered around scripture (the syna-gogue service) and the meal (the Lord's Supper). It was not one or the other—but always both. And the whole of the combined service reflected the conviction that the assembly met in honor of the risen Lord.

Word and Sacrament

Luke's Gospel (ch. 24) tells an Easter story that helps the reader understand the worship that developed in the early church. On the Sunday when the Marys and Peter had found Jesus' tomb to be empty, two followers of Jesus had been traveling. They were going from Jerusalem to a village called Emmaus. As they walked, they discussed what had happened in the past few days— Jesus' crucifixion, the disappointment of his disciples, and the rumor of an empty tomb. They were disturbed and puzzled. As they walked, a stranger joined them. (The reader knows that the stranger is Jesus, but the travelers didn't recognize him.) The stranger joins in the discussion. He cites various of the Hebrew scriptures (what we call the Old Testament) to interpret the Mes-siah's rejection, death, and vindication. No doubt the travelers found this discussion fascinating—as who wouldn't? When they came near the end of their journey, the two invited the stranger to share a meal. Luke tells us that "when he was at the table with them, he took bread, blessed and broke it, and gave it to them. Then their eyes were opened, and they recognized him. . . ."

When the stranger had vanished, and after they recovered from their astonishment, one said, "Were not our hearts burning within us while he was talking to us on the road, while he was opening the scriptures to us?" Tired as they must have been from their journey, they gathered their belongings and headed back to Jerusalem to report their experience. When they got back, "they told what had happened on the road, and how he had been made known to them in the breaking of the bread."

This is an important story not only for what it tells us about that particular Easter Sunday journey, but also for what it tells us about the worship of the early church. It highlights the two focal points of every Sunday service: the breaking of bread and the opening of the scriptures. The key figure in both of these events is the risen Lord. He "took bread, blessed and broke it, and gave it to them." At that point on the road to Emmaus, a remarkable thing had happened. "Then their eyes were opened, and they recognized him. . . ." Luke's message is that in the Lord's Supper—the taking, blessing, breaking, and giving of bread—the church meets the risen Lord over and over again. Jesus was "known to them in the breaking of the bread." But note also the reference to the scriptures. "Were not our hearts burning within us . . . while he was opening the scriptures to us?" Luke is affirming what the early Christians were discovering every time they assembled for worship—that the risen Lord made his presence known to them in the scriptures read and proclaimed and in the Lord's Supper. Jesus was, in fact, the host at each Sunday assembly. These traditions, stemming from the very earliest experience of the church, show us what New Testament scripture believed to be essential for the worshiping Christian community: Word (scripture read, interpreted, preached) and Sacrament (bread and wine taken, blessed, and shared). The point was that in Word and in Sacrament, the assembled congregation met the risen and living Lord. This sacred meeting is dramatically different from the experience of the mall or the theater.

Can We Relate to This?

For contemporary Protestants, in particular, it is generally easier to relate to the first part of early Christian worship—the synagogue service, or service of the Word. As Protestant worship has developed in North America, the sermon (or preaching of the Word) has taken the most prominent position. For various reasons, the Lord's Supper has been edged to the margins. But even if we have had no experience with preaching, we have other models that help us relate to it. Whoever has gone to school is familiar with classroom procedures. A teacher plays a prominent role. He or she is likely to stand before the class and speak. She may speak about the causes of the Civil War, or how to do long division, or he may explain how to diagram a sentence. Those who have gone to college, or watched a documentary on TV, also know what it's like to hear someone with recognized expertise present information. Candidates for office and advocates of good causes make pitches, trying to persuade their audiences to a particular point of view. It's not a huge leap from any of these experiences to the experience of hearing someone preach a sermon. We have ready models that make the giving of sermons somewhat understandable. Someone gives information, or makes an argument, or tries to persuade. Even those churches that distance themselves from tradition (and never use the words *sermon* or *preach*) nevertheless make use of something like a sermon. A verbal presentation of some kind persists in even the most radical of the new churches—even if accompanied by videos, slides, or drama. Whether they know it or not, this verbal presentation of the Christian faith has its roots in the Christian service of the Word, which in turn has roots in the synagogue service.

What many North Americans have a problem relating to is sacramental worship. Whether completely unfamiliar with churches or having a sketchy Protestant background, they have a hard time comprehending the point of this mini-meal of bread and wine (or crackers and grape juice). Teaching and learning, the advertising pitch, propaganda, passionately made arguments we can understand—but prayers over bread and wine, and their solemn distribution—what can this be about? It doesn't help much, either, to be told that the bread and cup represent the body and blood of Christ. The thought of it seems distasteful, if not downright spooky. It's not too hard to understand, then, why the seeker-oriented churches never have communion services. (Or, if they have them, don't have them on Sunday mornings but schedule them at separate times for the initiated.) While something like the sermon persists, the Lord's Supper seems a dispensable tradition—one that the contemporary service, as many call it, can easily leave behind.

Although even most unchurched people can relate to preaching, it may be that existing models don't really do justice to what preaching is intended to be and do. Is it instruction? Not really. A lecture on religious or moral topics? Not really. Is it a sales pitch? Not really. Is it an effort to argue or persuade? Not really. Is it meant to confront, threaten, scold? Not really. Is it an attempt to inspire religious feeling? Not really. And yet, in a way, preaching may do any or all of those things. Most of us are likely to put preaching in one of those little pigeonholes, but the fact is that there is more to it than can be contained in those categories. As we shall see later on, preaching is meant to be sacramental. In other words, to be a means by which Jesus Christ becomes present to his people. Because there are familiar models of public speaking, we may presume that we understand the preaching enterprise more than we really do. Yet we can profit from preaching even though we haven't precisely grasped its exact function.

The Lord's Supper is likely to be more puzzling to the uninitiated than is preaching. People are less likely to imagine that they have it figured out. Still, disciples of Christ can profit from the Lord's Supper even when they don't understand what it is meant to be or to do. It's always a relief to be able to understand things, but even things we're not entirely clear about can do their work in spite of our limitations.

Is It Reasonable?

Is it possible that the God revealed in Christ has intentionally chosen the means most profitably used by a congregation that gathers to worship in Christ's name? Worship is more than just a cafeteria of things we contrive to do because they seem religious. The aim of worship is not to teach or entertain or inspire (though all of those things may occur). The purpose of worship is to participate, as God may make it possible, in God's own life. God has shown us what we are to do to open ourselves to this participation.

The service that combines the Word (scripture read and proclaimed) and Sacrament (Holy Communion) has persisted, in one form or another, for many generations. At times, that service of Word and Sacrament has been distorted—one part or another disfigured or neglected. Nevertheless, the church has repeatedly returned to that model in times of renewal. Might there be wisdom in considering the possibility that there is strength in Word and Sacrament united, whether the worshipers fully understand their purpose and function or not? And that it might be premature—if not presumptuous—to discard one or the other solely on the grounds that their meaning is not obvious to those encountering them without prior experience? The style of the church's music, architecture, rites, and ceremonies has varied enormously over time and from place to place. The one consistency has been the persistent resort to these two primary means of worship. There is every reason to believe that God, wisely and graciously, has provided Christ's church with Word and Sacrament to guide us toward participation in God's own life.

How important is it to understand matters of the spirit? Some of us seem to be made in such a way that we need to process our experience through the intellect. Some are curious; some need reassurance; some need to sift and sort; some need to examine critically. Loving God with the mind might very well include putting ideas and claims to the test to separate the genuine from the false. Nevertheless, when we have gathered information, processed it thoroughly, and reached as much understanding as we're likely ever to reach, is it really possible to understand God? And if we could understand God, would God be God? Could we worship and serve a God whom we are capable of comprehending? I suspect that the true God will always be bigger than the grasp of the human mind. That surely doesn't mean that we should disengage our minds. It does suggest that if we are in any sense to know God, the mind may not be sufficient. Could it be that God may reach out to us in subtle ways, not independent of the conscious mind, but not entirely dependent on it, either?

Western society in the past 250 years has relied heavily on human reason to understand all sorts of things. The use of reason has helped to chase away superstition, puncture the pretensions of authorities who deliberately mystify, and clear the way for trial-and-error kinds of learning. Science and technology certainly owe a significant debt to the Western fascination with the rational. And yet the triumph of reason may also throw us off the track. It may cause us to neglect other aspects of our human being. If we distrust—and even shut down—that inner eye, inner ear, with which we discern the movement of God's Spirit, our rationality cannot make up for the loss.

Many mainline Protestant churches have not questioned our society's heavy reliance on the ability to explain everything from heredity to the market economy to the New Testament miracles. At church, we are content to sit quietly in rows and have the great mysteries explained to us. We are bewildered when people outside the church—particularly members of younger generations—are not so content. There is now more than one generation that is impatient with the project of trying to make God and God's ways understandable. Some of those generations are in rebellion against what seems to them to be the taming of the holy. They want to experience the holy—not have it explained to them. They want to be a part of it all—not absorb it second-hand. Churches with "seeker services" attempt to move their audiences with music, dramatic skits, and messages that offer solutions to problems of living. This caters to the wariness of the seeker, who wants to assess the Christian message from a distance. It's designed to appeal to seekers, and move them, without invading their space. Other "contemporary" styles of worship take exactly the opposite approach. They try to engage the worshiper, involving the worshiper deeply in praise and prayer.

The churches that have deliberately targeted unchurched young adults have designed their weekly assemblies to appeal to those who have not had a positive experience with traditional churches. In surveys, those young adults have reported that they do not feel at home in traditional churches. They can't relate to the architecture, the music, the formality, or the liturgy. In response to their needs, the churches created to reach out to them have supplied buildings and music that resemble the buildings and music of the secular culture. Congregations of seekers need be exposed to no churchly ritual, no mysterious symbols. It's possible to appreciate the motives and the creativity of these churches while questioning the product. Is the God of biblical faith a God who can be known or worshiped without symbol or rite? Or just any symbol or rite? Are Father, Son, and Holy Spirit a God who can be known or worshiped using only the vehicles of popular and commercial culture? At the same time, some mainline churches need to ask themselves whether they have made a routine out of the holy. Or imagined, too easily, that the things of God can be grasped by the ear and mind alone.

Feeding the Spirit

There is a strange inconsistency at work in North American society. Sally Fitzgerald has collected the letters of the twentieth-century novelist Flannery O'Connor under the title *The Habit of Being*. O'Connor, a devoted Catholic, reports in one of her letters her observation of young women in college sororities. O'Connor is intrigued at how much these sorority women love to produce various sorts of ceremonies that feature the lighting of candles. The novelist's point of view is that those who have never been exposed to the drama of worship have an unsatisfied appetite for it, so they cobble together rituals of their own. Watch the news-papers for similar phenomena. Candlelight vigils accompany all sorts of events, from protests outside the embassy of a country guilty of some oppression against its citizens, to street-corner gatherings in memory of a high school student killed by a drunken driver. There is a hunger for ritual among those who would never admit such a hunger. Painting one's face or body with the home team's colors and singing or chanting certain songs and cheers are among the rituals of college years. Young couples anticipating their own wedding eagerly collect rituals they have witnessed at other people's weddings—unity candles, readings, ritualized farewells to parents, music associated with occasions in the lives of the bride and groom. Every novelty is weighed and considered, and every time one is used, it's likely to be borrowed for still other weddings. And yet, if one were to point out to the couple that they are exhibiting a taste for ritual, many would deny it.

The same phenomenon was at work among the grandparents of these younger generations. Their grandparents belonged to the Masonic Lodge, the Eastern Star, the Odd Fellows, where there were rituals to be precisely observed. Very often at church no rituals were tolerated (insofar as they were recognized as rituals) or appreciated. But in the secrecy of the lodge, one could wear special clothing and follow rites that satisfied some hunger to which one would hardly confess at church. There was a playfulness in the rituals of the lodge that somehow seemed inappropriate in worship.

The truth is that there are inward experiences, dispositions, and relationships that can only be expressed symbolically—even playfully. Why is it that those who crave ritual (lighting matches or cigarette lighters at the end of rock concerts, for example) are unaware of the power of the liturgical drama? Why is it that a stripped-down version of Christian worship seems to play so well among those who, all their lives long, have been starved for something that cannot be expressed by words alone? It's possible that God's provision for us of Word and Sacrament is ideally suited to the complex beings that we are. It's possible that we may, in words and actions just beyond the horizons of understanding, meet the God who is always greater than the capacity of our minds to grasp. It's possible that our instinctive craving for ritual is part of our original equipment. Possible that God intends the sacramental drama to be a means by which God may meet us and touch us.

The first generation of Christians had not been trained to suppress those parts of themselves that could not be fitted into a box labeled "reasonable." They knew from scripture that they were to love God with heart, soul, and mind. They saw no incompatibility there. One encounters God with the heart—but that doesn't disconnect the mind. One encounters God with the soul—and neither does that unplug the intellect. One looks for God with the inquiring and discerning mind—but that doesn't disengage heart or soul. Heart, soul, and mind work together to bring us to a point of meeting with the God who *made* heart, soul, and mind—and who can approach us by all three routes. Those first Christians found that it was in Word and Sacrament that God engaged them in all these dimensions. The God who met them, and whom they met, in Word and Sacrament was none other than the One whom they had known as Father, Son, and Holy Spirit.

It's curious that the same society that produces churches stripped of traditional ceremony also produces New Age spirituality. Curious, also, that each aims at more or less the same population. One appeals to the need to demystify, and the other to the need for mystery. Many new congregations created for those disillusioned with traditional churches borrow from the secular culture the models of therapeutic speech and the concert. This culture gives all the appearance of straightforward rationality. On the other hand, the New Age movement, with its crystals, candles, angels, claims of multiple lives and out-of-body experiences, etc., gives no evidence of being constrained by reason.

Where there is no mystery—where even the most profound spiritual claims seem within the grasp of the intellect—the product is a certain barrenness. Where mystery is multiplied and cast loose from reason, there is likely to be superstition. The shape of Christian worship—the combination of Word and Sacrament—blends and balances the exercise of the mind with the nourishment of the soul. It challenges a barren rationality with mysteries that cannot be reduced to a logical argument. But it also requires mystery to be in touch with the mind's ability to absorb, weigh, evaluate, and encounter. The service of Word and Sacrament unites the capacity for thought with spiritual experience. It brings together what current fashions in spirituality are likely to break apart. But our generation is not the first to break apart what the first generation of Christians brought together.

3

What God Has United, One Must Not Divide!

Going to Church
with Aunt Millie and Uncle Don

*W*hen I was about twelve years old, my Aunt Millie and Uncle Don often invited me and others of their nieces and nephews to spend a week at their house. They lived about an hour's drive away from our home, but while we lived in a town, they lived in a city. Aunt Millie and Uncle Don had no children of their own. They enjoyed entertaining us, apparently, since we were thoroughly housebroken and wouldn't stay too long. Our parents seemed happy to have us spend a summer week with our aunt and uncle, but it was clear to me even as a child that the family had not entirely welcomed Uncle Don's wife. Although my parents belonged to a church, they rarely attended it. But Aunt Millie did go to church—a Catholic church. And, when she married my father's brother, he had become a Catholic, too! This, coupled with the fact that Aunt Millie came from somewhere "back east," created a certain amount of suspicion in my midwestern family.

When Sunday came, Aunt Millie was gracious enough to offer to drive us to the local Sunday school, which happened to be of the same denomination as the church we rarely attended. Horrified at the idea of being dropped into the midst of strangers our own age—and at having to go to Sunday school *in the summer!* —we chose the other option she offered—to go to Mass with her and Uncle Don. Aunt

Millie was determined to make a positive impression. The parish church apparently would not be good enough. She and Uncle Don drove us downtown, to the cathedral church, where we would experience Catholic worship for the first time. This was, bear in mind, before the Second Vatican Council. At that time, it was everywhere the case that the Catholic rite was recited in Latin. Aunt Millie proudly explained that one could visit any Catholic church in any country in the world and the Mass would be exactly the same.

The noon Mass at the cathedral was packed. There was no place for us in the pews. The sights and sounds swept over us, and we were awed by the kneeling, the sign of the cross, the holy water, the chanting of the choir, and the distant sound of an incomprehensible language. There was a sermon. Or, more accurately, a sort of gesture in the direction of a sermon. The priest rose to the pulpit and addressed the congregation. It seemed as though he was speaking without a plan. There was no evidence that he had crafted his sermon. His words were not far from what one might describe as a harangue—scolding those people who did not send their children to parochial school. After a few—what seemed to me incomprehensible—threats, this part of the service was over and we moved on to something else. It was brief enough that one could have stood on one foot the whole length of it. It seemed to me that something—although I could not identify what it might be—was missing.

Flash ahead several decades. The remarkable reforming Council, Vatican II, was long past. The Roman Catholic Church had experienced twenty years of change, including a beautiful effort to relate to other Christians—the so-called "separated brethren"—in a positive way. I was pastor of a Presbyterian congregation, and also active in ecumenical circles. I had invited a new friend—a Roman Catholic priest—to preach at our church. Although such a thing would have been unheard of twenty years before, he graciously accepted the invitation. The service that morning reached its climax in the sermon. Though Creed, prayers, Offertory, and hymns followed the sermon, there was no Lord's Supper. As my colleague and I took off our clerical robes, he said to me, "It always seems to me that there's something missing when there's no Eucharist" ("Eucharist" is one of the names for Holy Communion, or the Lord's Supper).

What's Missing?

In recent times, it is more likely that a person attending Catholic Mass will hear a real sermon—something crafted along the same order as a sermon preached in a Protestant church—but it's not inevitable. On the other hand, in most Protestant churches, Holy Communion is being celebrated far more frequently than it used to be. Nevertheless, chances are that unless the church is Episcopal—or possibly Lutheran—most Protestant services will include a sermon but no Lord's Supper. The Protestant visiting a neighbor's Catholic church still runs a high risk of missing anything resembling the sermon to which she or he is accustomed. And the Catholic visiting a relative's Protestant congregation runs at least as high a risk of missing the Sacrament (the Lord's Supper). If either visitor is more than an occasional churchgoer, she or he is likely to experience something missing in the other church. If Christian worship early on united in a single rite the synagogue service and the sacramental meal, how did we fall into this state of affairs? Where is the sermon at St. Mary's? And where is the Sacrament at Old First Church?

In the early centuries after Christ, Christianity knew nothing of an alternative between Protestant and Catholic. Although from time to time dissenting forms of Christianity emerged, the greater Church rejected them, and for the most part, they died out. For all practical purposes, there was one single Church, administered from several major centers. This one Church was surprisingly diverse—not as uniform as we may imagine it. Even its rites developed somewhat differently. Nevertheless, the basic shape of Christian worship continued in the pattern formed in the first generation. The Sunday service was one in which preaching and the Lord's Supper complemented one another. There was good preaching. In fact, there were a number of renowned preachers in those early centuries. Worship did not involve a choice between preaching and the Sacrament. Worship was, by definition, preaching and Sacrament combined in a single service—the normal weekly worship of the church—just as it had been in the earliest generations.

As the centuries passed, however, things changed. Preaching didn't die out completely, but it became rarer and rarer. Particularly in ordinary parish churches, preaching almost completely faded away. One reason may be that the church did not require much education for its priests. In fact, some could neither read nor write at all. They had learned the words, gestures, and actions of the Mass by heart, but had no profound understanding of the scriptures. Even if they could read, copies of the scriptures were not easily available in the era before the invention of the printing press. Bibles existed in the local languages, but most often they were written in Latin. Knowledge of the scriptures was clearly not a high priority. As preaching faded, claims about the Eucharist escalated. Merely being present as the Mass was being celebrated conferred spiritual benefits. These two trends reinforced each other. A heightened doctrine of Holy Communion had the effect of making preaching seem less important, and the reduction of preaching left a void that the church attempted to fill with exaggerated claims about the value of Holy Communion.

Going to Church before
the Protestant Reformation

What was it like going to church in the medieval period, on the eve of the Protestant Reformation (say, the early 1500s)? Christian people did not lose contact with the stories of the Bible. The stained-glass windows in the Gothic-style churches put the biblical stories before them. In addition, there were often magnificent paintings on the walls of the churches, providing a vivid reminder of the stories of Adam and Eve, Cain and Abel, Joseph, Mary, and the Child Jesus, and the whole range of biblical narratives. Statues of the Virgin, Jesus, and the saints brought them to life. To step inside a church would be to be surrounded by the great drama of the Bible, from beginning to end, in full color. There was

enough to absorb a worshiper's attention as she or he gazed upon
the work of painters, sculptors, stained-glass makers.

It was a good thing that the arts were available to occupy the
attention of those assembled. There were no printed orders of service, of course—nor were there missals—books in which one
could find a translation of the Latin service. Even if such things
had been available, few would have been able to read them. It
would have been difficult even to hear the service as spoken by
the priest. He was separated from the congregation by a high partition called a rood screen. The altar was hidden from view behind
it. It's likely that the people would have heard little more than a
low murmur. The congregation itself remained silent. There were
no sung or spoken responses. There were no hymns, except for
Latin hymns sung by a choir where there was one. Other than the
simple fact of their presence, the people played no role in the service. In fact, it was during the medieval period that someone
thought to invent the Rosary, so that those attending worship
would have something to do during the Mass. Using the Rosary
beads, they could pray and keep track of the number of their
prayers until they heard the ringing of the sanctuary bell.

At the crucial point in the service, the congregation would hear
the ringing of that bell from behind the rood screen. The sound of
the bell indicated that the priest had reached that point in the Mass
in which the bread and wine became the body and blood of Christ:
("This is my body"—in Latin, "Hoc est enim corpus meum,"
which the worshipers tended to hear as "hocus pocus"). It would
have been appropriate at that instant to genuflect (kneel briefly)
and make the sign of the cross.

When it was time to commune, the priest would offer the bread
to those who had prepared themselves by making their confes-
sions beforehand and receiving absolution. He did not offer the
cup. Since church authorities believed and taught that the bread
and wine became literally Christ's body and blood, it became too
dangerous to run the risk of spillage. Only the priest drank from
the cup. However, the great likelihood was that on any given Sunday, no one would go forward to receive communion anyway. The
people had become so awed by the Sacrament, and so anxious

about possibly dropping the wafer of bread or otherwise desecrating it, that they remained in their places. A church council, alarmed at this reticence, enacted a church law that required the faithful to take communion at least once a year, at Easter. So, though the practice of the medieval church was to celebrate Mass every Sunday (and, for that matter, several times every day), few actually communed.

Something Needed to Be Reformed

The service that had begun as a combination of the synagogue service and the meal had become something quite different. If the priest read scripture, it was in an unintelligible language. Preaching had fallen into disuse. The service of the Word (what had begun as the synagogue service) remained officially embedded in the text of the Mass, but for all practical purposes it may as well not have. There was—except rarely—no opportunity for the people to hear scripture read in a language they could understand, and no opportunity to hear it expounded in a sermon. The service of Word and Sacrament had been disfigured, with only the Sacrament side of it remaining. And even that began to look less and less like a meal. When preaching goes, the Sacrament will quickly lose its integrity. And, as we shall see, it works the other way, too.

It was during the 1500s that a well-educated monk became dissatisfied with the church as he observed and experienced it. His name was Martin Luther. Before the sixteenth century was over, several other church people—both priests and laypersons—had joined him in raising hard questions about current church practice and the theology that supported it. Those questions led to a movement of reform and church renewal that we call the Protestant Reformation.

Whenever there has been a time of reform and revitalization in the history of the church, one item high on the agenda has been the reform and revitalization of worship. This was true of that long and complicated period we call the Reformation, too. Martin Luther knew that there had to be changes, but he was conservative and approached the process of change carefully. A leader named John Calvin—not a priest but a layman—led the process of reform in the French-speaking Swiss cantons, centered in Geneva. Converted, apparently, by reading the writings of Luther, Calvin had been traveling through Geneva when local leaders drafted him to lead the reform of the church there. He consented, reluctantly. Calvin approached changes in worship less conservatively than Luther. Luther's influence contributed to the reshaping of worship in what came (against his will) to be called Lutheran churches. Calvin's influence contributed to the reshaping of worship in Reformed churches (today's Presbyterian, Congregational, and Reformed churches, and a number of Protestant bodies that stemmed from them or were formed in a milieu where their influence was dominant). In many respects, worship would have looked quite different in a Lutheran church than in one influenced by John Calvin. But certain things they had in common.

The new Protestant churches, by various names, agreed that worship ought to be in the language actually spoken by the people. Both Luther and Calvin took an interest in the history of worship and studied its development in the early centuries of the church. They agreed that the service of the Word, which had faded into insignificance, needed to be brought back to its rightful place. To that end, they restored the practice of reading scripture aloud in public worship in the local language. Alongside that, they reinstituted the practice of preaching and linked the sermon directly to the scripture read.

The Joy of Preaching!

The recovery of the service of the Word not only honored the Christian service as it had developed in the early church, but it also met an emerging need. A new middle class had appeared in the cities. The rising middle class, composed of merchants and entrepreneurs, were more literate than the rural population. They had developed a great curiosity about history, and origins, and how things had come to be. They were interested in classical literature, but their curiosity extended also to Christian origins—

and particularly to the Bible. Not long before, a man named Gutenberg had invented a system of printing that made it possible to reproduce multiple copies of a document easily and cheaply. Those who sought to reform the church could publish and circulate their own writings, but it also became possible for the first time for ordinary people to own their own copy of the scriptures. Access to the actual words of the Bible had a powerful effect and helped to create an enormous appetite to know more.

In addition, this new technology helped to shape a new way of thinking. Whereas people in the medieval period tended to think in images, the newly literate began to think in a linear fashion. Just as on the printed page one line follows another, so also one thought leads to another in linear progression. Although that may seem commonplace to us, it was a dramatic change that fundamentally reshaped the ways people learned to think and to communicate. The new literacy helped to stimulate a hunger for preaching. The recovery of the service of the Word combined with the new technology in a way that profoundly altered people's expectations of worship.

It so happens that neither Luther nor Calvin had any desire to elevate preaching at the expense of the Eucharist. Their intention was to restore what had been broken apart: the unity of Word and Sacrament—synagogue service and meal. In the process of renewing the worship life of the reforming churches, they wanted to add preaching—not subtract Holy Communion. If they had had their way, they would have reformed and renewed Protestant worship by recovering a balance between Word and Sacrament in every Sunday service.

The Reformers were not satisfied, however, with the Mass they had inherited from the medieval church. The first changes may have been architectural. The Reformers removed the rood screen—the partition that hid the altar and kept the people at a distance. In the Protestant churches, the Lord's Supper would be celebrated in the sight and hearing of the people. The churches most influenced by John Calvin removed the altars in existing churches and replaced them with simple Communion Tables. The idea was that the Lord's Supper would more nearly resemble a common meal. The presiding minister would stand behind the Holy Table, facing the congregation. In all Protestant churches, the Reformers restored the practice of giving the communicants both Bread and Cup. Sometimes, people came forward to the altar rail or Communion Table and knelt for communion. In other churches, they set up tables and chairs at which communicants came, by turns, to receive the Bread and Cup while seated. At other times, they stood at the Table. The intention was that the whole congregation—or very nearly so—would commune every time they celebrated the Lord's Supper. The service of the meal was not intended for isolated, self-selected individuals, but as a sign of the covenant that bound the entire congregation into a community of God's people.

A Failed Effort

The Protestant Reformers imagined a renewed worship to be a weekly service of Word and Sacrament—scripture read and preached plus Holy Communion. In Lutheran churches, the service differed little from the Mass except that they reduced and altered the Communion prayers and celebrated the service in the local language. In Reformed churches (those most influenced by Calvin), the service was much simpler, and also wordier. In both, congregations were expected to take an active part, particularly in congregational song. The Lutherans sang chorales and Latin hymns translated into German, while the Calvinists sang psalms and scriptural paraphrases. The Lutherans continued to use the old pipe organs, while the Calvinists sang unaccompanied. Despite differences in style, the intention of both was to bring back together what had been torn apart during the medieval period.

Unfortunately, they were not successful. Several powerful forces worked against them. For one, there was resistance to weekly communion. You will recall that in the medieval church, people seldom actually communed. Most worshipers would receive communion no oftener than once a year, when church law required it, at Easter. Although the priest had consecrated the bread and wine at every Mass—at least daily—nearly all church-goers had been merely spectators—or, more accurately, a distant audience. To leap from communing once a year to communing every Sunday was an enormous jump. There was a psychological barrier that resisted such dramatic change. At the same time, in spite of the teaching of the Reformers, the new Protestants retained a measure of the old fears of somehow—by dropping or spilling, perhaps—desecrating the consecrated bread and wine. To multiply that risk by fifty-two was too terrifying! The result was that the civil authorities that had the last word in the matter overruled the ecclesiastical authorities in the Reformed city of Geneva, and weekly communion never caught on elsewhere among Protestants in that era. In Geneva, Calvin's fallback goal became monthly communion, in which, of course, the whole con-gregation would share. But the secular authorities held firm, and the pattern became four times a year, at Christmas, Easter, Pente-cost, and early September. It was still two to four times more fre-quent than most people had communed before the Reformation, but it was a great disappointment to Calvin. He hoped that in time this practice, which he called "defective," would be improved.

There was another factor working against the recovery of a complete service of Word and Sacrament. Although the Protestant Reformers had made a break with Catholic belief and practice, more of it lingered than they recognized. In the late medieval period, on the eve of the Protestant Reformation, the Eucharist had acquired a sombre, penitential character. Devotion centered on the suffering Christ, abandoned by his disciples, bleeding and dying on the cross. The intention was that the devout should examine themselves, learn to deplore their sins, and beg for for-giveness. The Lord's Supper took its tone from the Last Supper that Jesus ate with his disciples before going to the cross.

This tone is quite different from the sense of a joyful recogni-tion of the presence of the risen Lord that had been a feature of the Lord's Supper as celebrated by the first Christians. Somehow, the Protestant Reformers, in their study of worship in the early church, had not been able to rise above the piety they had learned and absorbed in the church of their childhoods. Protestant worship introduced a different practice of the Lord's Supper and a different way of understanding it. However, it carried with it the same dark, penitential mood. Some have described it as a "funeral for Jesus." It's no surprise, then, that the new Protestants recoiled at the idea of reliving Jesus' suffering every Sunday. The fact that the service would be spoken clearly in their own language might have made it worse than had it been spoken in a foreign language, barely audible!

In later generations, in places like Scotland, this same penitential theme would prevail. In fact, the association of communion with self-examination and penitence became so pronounced that the Scottish churches celebrated the Lord's Supper even less frequently than in Geneva—no more than once or twice a year. The penitential theme had led to the institution of preparatory services before every communion service, centered on confession of sin. The communion season in a particular parish involved elaborate preparation, including not only the preparatory services, but the examination of each potential communicant by the elders of the church. The infrequent communion seasons often drew crowds. People came from neighboring parishes. The crowds were frequently large enough that the services would be held outdoors, the communicants taking turns sitting at a table prepared for that purpose. Often the service would be preceded by a number of sermons, sometimes by several preachers. This Scottish communion season became, in America, the framework around which open-air revival meetings developed. The penitential tone and the elaborateness of the preparation required kept scheduled communions infrequent. Nevertheless, these communion seasons attracted individuals who might very well travel to other parishes for them, so that some church members might have communed more frequently than their own congregations would have made possible.

There is a direct link, however, between the penitential tone of the service and its infrequency. The result was that in most Protestant churches influenced by Scottish practice, the Lord's Supper became occasional. Ironically, the Protestant Reformers' goal of restoring the broken unity of Word and Sacrament came undone. Only this time, it wasn't preaching that was marginalized. This time, it was the Lord's Supper.

A Marginalized Sacrament

Apart from these handicaps, the Reformers' vision would have had a hard time being maintained on American soil. The Lord's Supper requires an ordained minister to preside. It's not a question of supernatural powers. The presiding minister, by virtue of ordination, acts as a representative of the whole church. To require a representative church officer to preside is a symbolic way of saying that Christ has entrusted the Lord's Supper to the whole church rather than to individuals. However, on the American frontier, ordained ministers were in short supply. Christians—and whole congregations—often relied on circuit riders—itinerant preachers—who visited occasionally. It was possible for groups to gather and sing hymns, pray, and read scripture without an ordained minister—and perhaps one member might even be gifted enough to expound the scripture. Although the churches might have conceived of some *interim* arrangement to make the Lord's Supper possible, they did not. Except for the Disciples of Christ, who discarded the whole idea of a representative officer, it was not feasible for Protestant churches to celebrate the Lord's Supper frequently—much less weekly. The weekly sermon was the staple of Protestant worship, and practical necessity combined with history to continue to marginalize the Lord's Supper.

If you were to stand outside a Presbyterian, Baptist, or Methodist church today and ask departing members why they don't have communion every Sunday, what do you think they would answer? Some would certainly confess that they don't have a clue! Others would claim that it's a matter of principle. "It's more meaningful," they might say. "To have it too often would make it ordinary." The truth, however, is that infrequency of communion is not rooted in some principle zealously adhered to by Protestants. Infrequency of communion—the marginalization of the Lord's Supper—can be traced to historical circumstance. Such infrequency was not the intention of those who led the church renewal movement we know as the Reformation. They visualized the reuniting of the two essential pieces of Christian worship—preaching and the Lord's Supper. However, although they were remarkably and astonishingly successful in restoring the place of preaching, their project of restoring Word and Sacrament as the ordinary Sunday service failed. We are still burdened, in many cases, by the tendency to identify the Lord's Supper with Jesus' *Last* Supper—with suffering and loss and sin. And, quite practically, it's also a fact that when congregations celebrate the Lord's Supper infrequently, the mechanics of it make us anxious every time. Those who serve it wonder, "Now, where do I stand? What comes first?" Similarly, the congregation worries, "What am I supposed to do?" Something that has to be learned all over again nearly every time requires us to pay too much attention to the details. The nourishment offered becomes obscured by fussing over the how-tos.

Putting the Word at Risk

When we break apart Word and Sacrament, we violate more than historical precedents. The example of the medieval church illustrates how the Sacrament, without the Word, can easily slide into superstition. However, it's equally true that the Word, without the Sacrament, can lose its essential character, too. At the time of the Protestant Reformation, when Protestants first recovered strong preaching, the preachers seemed to have a clear idea of their task. First of all, it was required that they be well educated in theology and the scriptures—including study of scripture in the original languages, Hebrew and Greek. They understood the work of preaching to be the opening up of the scriptures so that the Lord of the scriptures might speak to the people. It was clear that scripture and sermon were meant to be intimately related. The reading of scripture immediately preceded the sermon as an indication that one flowed from the other. The preacher's task was not to moralize—to find some tidbit of commonsense wisdom—but, having studied the scripture and wrestled with its meaning, to pass on to the congregation what the scripture said about God and God's work in the world and what God called God's people to do.

Even in those first generations during which the recovery of preaching had been thought out so carefully, it may be that preachers fell short of the ideal more often than not. But there was a certain confidence and clarity among those who had had to deal with the significance of the restoration of the service of the Word. It's hard to tell how long it may have been before those called to preach began to lose sight of the original vision. We know that as intellectual fashions changed, preaching began to change as well. Frank Senn reports on some German Lutheran sermons in the 1700s. One minister, preaching from Luke 24 (the story of Jesus' appearance on the road to Emmaus—a story of exceptional nuance and depth) managed to transform it into a superficial exhortation. The theme of his sermon was that going for walks was a healthful exercise.

Such deterioration of preaching might have occurred under any circumstances, but the infrequency of the Lord's Supper contributes to a distortion of preaching. The presence of the Sacramental celebration in a service directs the congregation toward the altar or the Communion Table. The altar/table fixes attention on God and God's gift to us in Jesus Christ, brought into the present by the power of the Holy Spirit. The Lord's Supper is clearly about God, and God's action in Christ. When there is no Lord's Supper to anchor the congregation in Christ, it becomes far easier for preaching to become detached from Christ.

Preaching has, from the eighteenth century forward, often and in many places become mistaken for an academic exercise—a lecture on some religious topic. Preaching has often left scripture behind. It is still not unusual to find Protestant services in which the reading of scripture and the sermon occur at widely separated points in the service, as though one had no relation to the other. And, in fact, it has frequently been unclear that there is—or should be—any relation between the two.

Topical preaching may be only loosely attached to scripture. Preachers may use the sermon to teach a doctrine; or to offer guidance on marriage, child-raising, handling conflict, or being effective in the workplace. They may conceive it as therapy or as a motivational speech. In some churches, preaching serves almost no purpose except to try to make new converts, or to stir up an emotional response. Preachers may use their sermons to instruct their congregations on race relations, economic justice, or making public places accessible to the disabled. There are even churches in which the sermon often rallies the troops around a political movement—perhaps summoning the congregation to support the pro-life movement or to oppose civil rights for homosexuals, or to vote as a bloc in opposition to or support of certain candidates.

Some denominations note on their official calendars various themes presumably to be celebrated in Sunday services: AIDS Awareness Sunday, World Order Sunday, etc. Perhaps you have had the experience—as I have—of attending worship on Scout Sunday, when a recital of the benefits of scouting has replaced the sermon. Whoever came to church desperate for a word from the Lord had to do without. Other denominations send out liturgical materials and suggested biblical texts to support various themes to be lifted up in prayers, litanies, and sermons.

A Dynamic Tension

This development is lamentable, not because those who preach should never speak of various commendable causes, but because such preaching begins with a topic or a point to be made, and only later searches scripture for some verses to support it. Such preaching runs the risk of turning into propaganda—even though it may be good and healthy and absolutely true propaganda. Propaganda and preaching are not the same thing. Preaching that is true to the gospel must always be rooted in scripture, shaped and formed by scripture first of all. Only when it is rooted in scripture can preaching be rooted in Christ. No method can guarantee that a sermon will truly draw its vitality from scripture, but it is far more likely to happen when preaching occurs regularly in balance with the celebration of Holy Communion. The Lord's Supper will not let us forget the Christ who is our foundation—the Christ we come to know in his past and in our present, and whom we expect to meet in the future. There is a dynamic tension between preaching and Sacrament that keeps each one true to itself. The Holy Spirit resists human efforts to pull apart what God has joined together. It is only with peril that we divide them.

4

Baptism—The Church's Front Door

Who Gets Baptized?

*I*n our church, like many others, we ask those present at worship to record their attendance on what we call the Fellowship Pad. Visitors and members alike write their names, addresses, phone numbers—and then they check a box labeled "Member" or "Visitor." When I check the pads on Sunday after church, I see that Melanie or David has checked "Visitor," even though the minister who preceded me baptized both of them when they were a few months old. When David began the Confirmation Class last year, he still checked "Visitor." But, in the box labeled "Member," he's started to write "almost!" Are our baptized children merely visitors at church?

How does one become a Christian? Is it by a decisive conversion experience? Is it by a gradual shift in perspective that reaches a climax in a firm commitment? Can a person always be a Christian—never having any conscious awareness of being anything but a believer? The answer to all three questions is "Yes." Some people meet Christ as suddenly as though they had turned a city street corner and nearly collided with another pedestrian. Some mull over the options, wrestle with questions, move toward tentative conclusions and then retreat, at last reaching a settled place where they have made up their minds. Others, raised by Christian parents, embrace the faith that has surrounded them, supported them, and stimulated their growth since earliest childhood. There is more than one way to become a Christian, but all enter the church through the door of baptism.

Some folks come to faith, with baptism following. In other cases, parents carry their infant children to church for baptism, followed by nurture and education that lead to faith. Of course, there are no guarantees. As in the parable of the sower (Mark 4:13–19), some of those who come to faith as adults lose that faith. And some who are nurtured in it from infancy lose it as well. There have always been those who trusted Jesus, and then changed their minds. Even some who knew Jesus personally "turned back and no longer went about with him" (John 6:66). There are disappointments, of course, but the grand thing is that faith takes root and flourishes generation after generation—sometimes where we least expect it. Whether faith precedes baptism or, in the case of children of believers, follows baptism, baptism is the door to the church. David, a new member of the Confirmation Class, is not "almost" a member. Since his baptism, he has been a member of the church, the intergenerational community gathered around Jesus Christ. From early childhood, he has been welcomed at the Communion Table. Now, in Confirmation Class, he is not debating whether or not to join the church. He is weighing whether he is ready for the first time to profess in public the faith he has always known, and how he might follow through with it as he grows into mature discipleship.

Who gets baptized? The New Testament says nothing about infant baptism. The Baptists have been saying that for a long time, and they are, of course, right. (Also, Seventh-Day Adventists, Assembly of God members, Disciples of Christ, Church of the Brethren Congregants, Churches of Christ folks, Mennonites, etc.) According to the biblical record, whom did the early church baptize? It's clear enough: they baptized adult converts. Adult converts were people who had heard the gospel message, responded to it positively, and sought entrance into the church.

If the biblical record is so clear, why don't all churches baptize adult converts? The answer is, they do. Roman Catholics, Presbyterians, Lutherans, Methodists, Baptists all baptize unbaptized adults who come to faith and seek membership in the church. The difference of opinion is on what to do about the *children* of adult converts—as well as the children of long-standing church members.

The New Testament does not record any baptism of an infant or child. It does record instances in which entire households are baptized along with the adult convert who heads the family. Perhaps those extended households included children, but scripture does not offer enough information for us to know that for sure. With no direct New Testament evidence for infant baptism, aren't those churches right that withhold baptism from their children until they are old enough to make their own confession of faith? That would seem to be a logical conclusion, except for one thing. The New Testament does not record a single instance of baptizing anyone whose parent was already a member of the church. There is no biblical account of the baptism of an eight-year-old, or a twelve-year-old, or a fifteen- or twenty-year-old daughter or son of church members. If the New Testament is silent about the *infant* children of church members, it is also silent about the *mature* children of church members. In either case, scripture is simply silent. Although every Christian church can agree on the baptism of adult converts, scripture gives no direct answer to the question of when their children may be baptized. To settle that question, it's necessary to look more closely at what baptism means and also to try to put ourselves in the place of those first Christians to see if we can imagine the development of their thinking about this matter.

Should we consider our children to be *out* of the community of faith until they deliberately and self-consciously choose to be *in*? Or should we consider them *in* until they may, perhaps, choose to be *out*? Once they began having children, those first converts to the Christian faith would have had to have dealt with exactly that question. If we are to get into the minds of that first generation, it's necessary first of all to recall that they were, for the most part, Jewish Christians. Jews also produced children, and it is quite evident that they considered their children to be *in*—members of the community of Israel—from birth. While Jewish adults sometimes did fall away from the faith of Israel, and followed some other faith, Jews did not conclude that they should postpone entrance rites until their children were old enough to make a mature, lifetime choice.

In the neighborhood where my family lives, most folks have at one time or another been invited to attend a *bris*. A *bris* is the ritual act of circumcision, performed according to Jewish law on the eighth day after the birth of a son. In the case of little girls, Jewish parents take their daughters to the synagogue for blessing and naming. The Jewish community counts both boys and girls as members from birth. Whatever path they may take as adults, Jewish children are not somehow set adrift from the community until they are mature enough to choose it. Jewish children share the same community as their parents. Neither Jews nor early Christians understood themselves or their children as free-floating individuals, unanchored to other people. Israel understood herself to be in a *covenant* relationship with God. A covenant is a solemn contract or agreement. In Israel's case, there were two partners to the covenant—God and the people. God had spelled out the terms of the contract, each partner having an obligation to the other: "I will be your God. You will be my people." The "you" of the covenant included not only grownups but also their offspring. Jewish children were *in*. This is the background that would have formed the thought of the first Jewish Christians when they considered the status of their children in relation to the people of the *new* covenant—the church.

Please notice that the issue was *their own* children—not children in general. The question is not, Should infants and children be baptized? The question is, Should *children of church members* be baptized? We know what the decision was, although we do not know when the church made the decision or how it made it. There is no record of any conflict over the matter, or of a debate leading to resolution. All that we know is that the church from as early as the second century actually baptized the infant children of church members. That practice became the normative practice of the church until some people caught up in church reform reopened the whole question at the time of the Protestant Reformation. The vast majority of Protestants, along with Catholics and Orthodox, have continued to baptize the dependent offspring of church members.

Which Children Are Eligible for Baptism?

Last Sunday, when Matt and Melissa brought their daughter to be baptized, the presiding minister read from the baptism service this requirement, and addressed it to them: "As God embraces you within the covenant, I ask you to reject sin, to profess your faith in Christ Jesus, and to confess the faith of the church, the faith in which we baptize." Then, she asked Matt and Melissa to turn from the ways of sin and to "renounce evil and its power in the world." The next question was, "Do you turn to Jesus Christ and accept him as your Lord and Savior, trusting in his grace and love?" When they responded affirmatively, the minister asked, "Will you be Christ's faithful disciple, obeying his Word and showing his love?"

The church requires that Matt and Melissa answer these questions for themselves. There is no pretense that they are answering them on Grace's behalf. We do not baptize children whose parents have no relation to the church. Baptism does not automatically confer some spiritual benefit in and of itself. Baptism can bear fruit in a child's life only when church and parents in concert teach that child how to claim those benefits. That is not possible unless the parents have a living relationship with the community of faith—a particular Christian congregation. A child will not experience that living relationship if its parents—or guardians—have none.

Changes in North American society pose a problem to our practice of baptism. The problem today stems from the fact that many people remember a connection with the Christian church even though they have allowed that relation to lapse. The vast majority of people in North America have at least some ancestral connection to Christianity. In earlier generations, it might have been reasonable to expect that one's children, raised in the church, would also raise their own children in the church. That's not true today.

And yet, in our society, the birth of children still seems to call for baptism, whether the parents of the child have any faith or not; whether the faith they may have is the faith of the church, or not. Parents who have forsaken any church connection expect that they are obligated to have their children baptized. Or, if not obligated, they see baptism as a kind of insurance policy against some peril in this life or the next—or they see it as a celebration of childbirth, or a naming ceremony with no particular religious significance.

Even more often, grandparents expect to see their grandchildren baptized, according to custom, even though their own offspring—the parents of the newborn—have only a nostalgic relation to the church and its faith. It's not uncommon, then, for churches to have to face the dilemma of what to do when there is a request to baptize a child whose parents have no intention of relating to the church. If the church consents, it encourages parents to make public vows they do not mean or intend to keep, and it contributes to distorted notions of what baptism is. In these circumstances, the church forfeits the right to define the meaning of its own sacraments, and determine who is eligible to receive them.

What do we do when there is an inappropriate request for the baptism of a child whose parents have no current relationship with the church? If the church responds that it cannot baptize such a child until the parents have established membership in a congregation, it may hurt the feelings or incur the wrath of well-meaning grandparents who don't know what the church's teaching about baptism is, and do not realize how radically society has changed in a generation or two. If it caves in, the church compromises the integrity of the sacrament and its own integrity by requiring solemn promises of people who it well knows have no intention of keeping them. It also teaches the congregation that they need not take seriously the promises they make "to guide and nurture" a child "by word and deed, with love and prayer, encouraging them to know and follow Christ and to be faithful members of his church." Why should they take such promises seriously when it's clear in advance that neither they nor any other congregation will have any access to this child, whose parents desire no relationship with the church? When a parent (or grandparent) makes an inappropriate request for baptism, the church's responsibility is to guide them carefully and prayerfully to put first what belongs first: settling the question of the parent's own commitment and membership.

Can An Unbaptized Child Go to Heaven?

This is the wrong question. Baptism is not about who goes to heaven and who doesn't. Our church does not teach that unbaptized people are outside of God's love. We do not claim that God loves only church members. Baptism is not some species of magic, that forces God's hand, requiring God to open the gates of heaven to whoever has received the sacrament. Nor does the lack of baptism restrain God from loving and redeeming whomever God pleases. Rather, in the sacrament of baptism, the Holy Spirit grafts us—mature person or babe in arms—to the body of Christ. The sacrament takes place in a context that includes Christ, the church, the person baptized, and in the case of children, parents. The Spirit is at work in that whole milieu to join us to Christ and Christ's people. In baptism, God does not choose us to be the only ones who have any hope of heaven. God chooses us to be "marked as Christ's own forever," a member of a people appointed for special service.

If God has chosen us, for what have we been chosen? Has God chosen to love us, and not to love others? Has God chosen to redeem us, and not others? Has God chosen to open the gates of eternal life to us, and not to others? That's not what we mean when we use the word chosen. God has chosen us to be a part of God's servant-community. People have heard that the Jews believe themselves to be God's chosen people. Many have resented that, presuming that it arises out of some conceit. But the Old Testament does not understand chosenness as superiority. The chosen people are not above others. God chose the people of Israel for a particular purpose—that through their service in the world, they might testify to the reality of God and God's claims upon all people, and in that way become a blessing "to all the families of the earth" (Gen. 12:3).

Christians, too, understand themselves to be chosen. In our

case as well, God has not chosen us to lord it over others, or to have an exclusive claim on God's love. God has chosen us, in Christ, for special service. Scripture says of the church, "But you are a chosen race, a royal priesthood, a holy nation, God's own people, *in order that you may proclaim the mighty acts of him who called you out of darkness into his marvelous light*" (1 Pet. 2:9). When God chooses us, God enlists us, ordains us, and equips us to be part of a priestly people, having the interests of the whole world at heart. It is not true that God loves only the baptized, or only those with a robust faith. The work God chooses us to do is to exhibit God's wide-ranging love in the places where we live, work, vote, think, discuss, choose allies, and act. "For God so loved *the world* that he gave his only Son . . ." (John 3:16).

Who's Choosing Whom?

When I was ten years old, the church my family belonged to announced the formation of a Pastor's Class for those to be baptized on Palm Sunday. My parents were ambivalent about the church. Sensing that, I found that I could usually manipulate my mother when it came to going to Sunday school, youth groups, and—in this instance—the Pastor's Class. I put up resistance, and managed to avoid going. Nevertheless, class or no class, it was expected that I would follow the protocol, and I did. On Palm Sunday, the minister asked me to make a profession of faith in Jesus Christ. Although I remember distinctly that I did not believe what I had been asked to affirm, I knew the "correct" answer and provided it. "Believer's" baptism followed.

The church of my childhood did not believe in or practice infant baptism. Nevertheless, at the age of ten the church considered that we were old enough to make a solemn commitment to discipleship. It probably works that way for some, but no scheme about how things should work is perfect. The truth is that my baptism meant nothing to me at the time. To our minister, it may have looked as though I had chosen Jesus Christ (or maybe he'd been around the track enough times to suspect that it didn't always happen that way). In any case, that was the way it was supposed to work in our church. We were the ones doing the choosing. In my case, it just didn't happen to apply.

If baptism results from someone's having chosen Jesus Christ, what does baptism mean when the person being baptized has only pretended to make such a choice? What was the real significance of my baptism? Since in fact I had not chosen Jesus Christ, does that mean that my baptism was meaningless? Should it have been repeated when the time came that I really did choose Jesus Christ? And should it perhaps be repeated again—and maybe again—whenever I cross some new threshold of maturity? Whenever I choose Christ more surely, more firmly, more forcefully than the last time?

Of course, an adult coming to faith for the first time does choose Jesus Christ, and choose to be baptized. But that choosing may obscure the fact that something else is at work here, too. I can't remember when it was that I first noticed and was struck by these words that Jesus spoke to his disciples: "You did not choose me but I chose you" (John 15:16).

In the case of the disciples, that choosing is perfectly obvious when we read the Gospels. Jesus had walked along the shore of the Sea of Galilee. He had seen men out fishing, or mending their nets, and called them to come join him in his mission. This choosing was quite different from the way things usually worked in those times. If someone wanted to learn from a teacher (a rabbi), that person had to approach the teacher and ask to be taken on as a student or an apprentice. In the case of Jesus and his disciples, the initiative came from exactly the opposite direction. Jesus made the first move. So, his statement to the disciples was quite literally true: "You did not choose me but I chose you."

The God whom we know in Christ similarly makes the first move. It may seem to the adult convert that he or she is the one who has done all the choosing. But on reflection, it seems rather that God has been at work in our lives since before we were looking for God, or in a position to choose one way or another. Jesus told a story about a shepherd who had a hundred sheep to take care of. At the end of the day, it was the shepherd's job to guide the sheep back to the shelter of their fold. Before securing them

for the night, the shepherd had to take inventory. Counting carefully, he discovered that there were only ninety-nine sheep. One
was missing. The story doesn't tell us anything about the circumstances, but quite possibly the missing sheep had no fear or anxiety at all. It may have been quite content to continue munching
the green grass, without even noticing that it had been separated
from the others.

In Jesus' story, the shepherd goes out to search for the lost
sheep. When he finds it, he tenderly lifts it to his shoulders and
carries it back to the shelter of the flock. This story is about God's
ways with us. It wasn't the sheep who went looking for the shepherd. God comes searching for us—even when we are entirely
oblivious to the fact that we need to be found. God refuses to stop
looking until God finds us. Even if the sheep had become aware
of its separation from the others, and begun to look around to see
if she could find them, the shepherd had already set out in search.
We may choose God. But behind our choosing is God's choosing.
"You did not choose me but I chose you. And I appointed you that
you should go and bear fruit. . . ."

In the case of my own baptism, it would not be true to say that
no choosing was going on just because I had not, in fact, chosen
to be Christ's disciple. There was some choosing going on, but it
was not my choosing. It was God's choosing. So my baptism was
not a meaningless gesture. It had meaning, although that meaning
was nowhere in evidence to me at the time. It would become evident when the time came that I would choose back the God who
had already chosen me. God's choosing is at work in the baptism
of adults, and also in the baptism of infants. In the case of adults,
we presume that they have responded positively to the gracious
invitation of the choosing God. In the case of the infant children
of Christians, we trust God to work through the family and church
relationship, choosing to add children of the covenant to the
household of God. The fact that a child brings absolutely nothing
to baptism points back to God's action, God's choosing, God's
movement toward us long before we are prepared to move toward
God. The church's duty, then, in concert with parents, is to coach
each child to the point where he or she may choose back—again
and again—the God who first chose the child.

When I reached the point of choosing back the God who had chosen me, I claimed my baptism and made it my own. It was not necessary to ask to have it done over again. That's because it was not my choosing that played the crucial role in my baptism. It was God's choosing. And God's choosing was not a fickle choice, or an uncertain choice, or a choice that had no force when at first I did not return it. My baptism stood as a monument not to my choosing, but to God's. God's promise—to be my God, and to make a place for me among God's people—was absolutely reliable.

To have attempted to repeat my baptism would have been to cast doubt on God's promise and its reliability. For that reason, the church does not repeat baptisms, no matter how much a person may imagine that he or she might improve upon the original one. However, many churches do provide periodic opportunities for members of congregations to reaffirm their baptismal covenant. Often this may be done on the Sunday that commemorates the Baptism of the Lord, or at an Easter vigil. Provisions may be made as well for individuals to reaffirm their baptismal covenant at moments when they feel called to a more profound discipleship. Such services offer the opportunity to reaffirm the faith of the church and often to receive the laying on of hands or anointing with oil.

"Unless I wash you. . . ."

Baptism is best understood as a gift. Whether for an adult or for a dependent child, baptism represents God's freedom to choose whomever God will choose. E. Schillebeeckx has compared baptism to a parent's kiss. Parents love their newborn child, and hold it and cuddle it and kiss it. In time, the child, having felt the power of the parents' love, learns at first to hug back, and then to return a kiss for a kiss. The television newsmagazines have shown us pictures of orphaned children, abandoned in institutions where there are not enough caregivers. Deprived of an adequate diet of love, children may fail to thrive, and eventually die. Those who survive will grow up emotionally disfigured, unable to love. To be a loving person, one must first know what it is to be loved. In the

case of baptism, the sacrament represents God's love, which sur-
rounds us, embraces us, upholds us even before we are capable of
recognizing it or returning it. But it's God's love for us that
enables our ability to love God in return.

Certainly, God loves children and adults who are not baptized,
and who know nothing of God, or who worship false gods. But
baptism is for us a tangible sign of God's love, which may not
belong to us exclusively, but includes us really and personally.
Baptism, then, is a gift to be welcomed and cherished. In the case
of an adult, the adult brings faith to her or his baptism. In the case
of a child, the child comes empty-handed. The child's empty-
handedness vividly illustrates what is true in either case: it's
God's giving that is the decisive act.

In John's account of Jesus' last meal with his disciples, he
records a scene in which Jesus pours water into a basin and begins
to wash each of the disciples' feet in turn. When he comes to
Peter, Peter objects. After all, it's a humble act to wash the feet of
a guest. That sort of thing should be done by a servant. At the very
least, Peter could wash his own feet and would prefer to do it than
see his Lord take on this menial role. To Peter's objection Jesus
replies, "Unless I wash you, you have no share with me." This text
has been commonly understood to refer, though indirectly, to baptism. Peter, getting the point for once, said, "Lord, not my feet
only but also my hands and my head!" In a sacramental way, baptism represents the promise that Christ will cleanse us. This particular washing is not a do-it-yourself project. It's Christ who baptizes. Our place is to accept the washing he offers. Baptism is his
work, his gift, ours to receive.

However, to us who receive this gift he also hands a basin and
a towel that are part of the church's equipment for service. Baptism unites us with him who takes the servant role. We who have
been washed become washers of feet, offering relief to the road-
weary—to those who are worn and dirty from the length and dif-
ficulty of their journey in the world. The servant-church lifts up
the cause of the poor, cares for the wounded and abandoned in
their distress, sends food to the hungry, and digs wells for the
thirsty. It builds Habitat houses; staffs soup kitchens; provides

warm clothing to the homeless; sends missionary doctors, nurses, teachers, and agricultural specialists; and appeals to the powerful who are in a position to reshape the warped places in the law to provide for those who cry out for justice. It opens day-care centers, nursery schools, and hospices. It speaks up for the voiceless and carries heartfelt messages from one corner of the world to the other and back again. This is our footwashing, our towel-and-basin service. This is how we add our small effort toward the blessing of "all the families of the earth."

Baptized—*in Water*

In our church, when we baptize, we first pour a lot of water from a large pitcher into the baptismal font. The minister holds the pitcher up high so that the whole congregation can see the water flowing and hear it splashing. When the minister baptizes, she takes great handfuls of water and applies it to the head of the person being baptized. Sometimes, suits and dresses and baptismal gowns get soaked. Couldn't God do without the water? I'm sure the Spirit doesn't depend on the use of water in baptism, but nevertheless Christ has chosen to attach his name and his promise to baptism in water. We can't see or touch the Holy Spirit, but we can see and touch the water. God graciously provides for our need for some concrete thing to represent the action of the invisible Spirit.

When I was a seminary student, a teacher told us that if we should ever find ourselves needing to baptize someone while marooned in a desert, we could baptize with sand. While I don't doubt that such a baptism would be better than nothing, the occasion has never arisen. But in baptism, except in those extreme circumstances, it's not sand that represents the Spirit, but water. Water, which flows where it will, as the Spirit does.

Why did Christ see fit to hallow ordinary water for this special purpose? It may be because baptism is intimately associated with new life in Christ, and water is inescapably associated with life. Without water, the planet earth would be lifeless. Even our own bodies are largely composed of water—over 90 percent. Where there is no water, there is desolation. Those who live in dry climates, like the ancient Israelites and the early Christians, are among the first to testify to the intimate association between water and life. No wonder, then, that the water of baptism provides a potent symbol of the new life that springs up in Christ.

Whenever we baptize, the presiding minister offers a Prayer of Thanksgiving over the water. The prayer alludes to the watery chaos over which the Spirit moved before God created the heavens and the earth (Gen. 1:1). The minister may pray, "In the time of Noah, you destroyed evil by the waters of the flood, giving righteousness a new beginning." The prayer evokes the time when God led Israel safely through the waters of the Red Sea, saving her from a destroying army. And in the prayer the congregation recalls Jesus' own baptism by John in the waters of the Jordan River.

Why does our baptismal prayer recall all these ancient things? Because we remember each of these events as times of new beginnings. Over, under, through, and in the waters God has done a new thing. It is just so with those who are baptized. God's Spirit is at work in our baptism to begin a new thing in us. The water of baptism is a vivid reminder of the ancient stories whose theme is that our God is a God of new beginnings.

In the Prayer of Thanksgiving over the water, the minister thanks God for the water of baptism, in which "we are buried with Christ in his death." From New Testament times, baptism was understood to be a union with Christ in his death. Baptism carries us, however young and vigorous we may be, to that borderline between death and life. Baptism is a symbolic drowning of the old self, the self who imagines that it's possible to be self-sufficient, the imperial self who insists on being in control at all times. In the case of an adult who may have lived a rebellious or an indifferent life, devoted only to his or her own pleasures, this drowning of the old self clearly marks a turning point. In the case of an infant or young child, this sacramental and symbolic drowning requires us to exercise our imaginations. After all, the child hasn't had a chance to mess up her or his own life. And maybe she won't. Nevertheless, baptism represents the drowning of the natural self, the self-absorbed self we begin to form as soon as we become conscious of the fact that what we want may put us in conflict with others. In baptism, the church acts out its prayer for us, that those impulses that set us against God and our neighbor may be drowned over and over again, laid to rest, and buried.

The prayer over the baptismal water moves from death to resurrection. United to Christ and to the whole body of Christ, we are confident to expect new life to spring up. In the act of baptism by immersion, the minister plunges the adult or the infant (as in Eastern Orthodox churches) beneath the waters and raises them out of it again. "For if we have been united with him in a death like his, we will certainly be united with him in a resurrection like his" (Rom. 6:4,5). Another prayer over the baptismal water is "Pour out your Spirit upon us and upon this water, that this font may be your womb of new birth." The unborn child *in utero* swims in amniotic fluid. Sheltered and nourished in the womb, the soon-to-be child grows toward his or her new life. Quietly, God is at work to shape what she or he will become. Baptism is also womb-like, in that, in a sacramental and symbolic way, the baptismal waters mark the onset of our formation as new creatures in Christ.

The pouring of water upon the baptized person resembles the outpouring of the Spirit. In the book of the prophet Joel, God said, "I will pour out my spirit on all flesh. . . ." The sprinkling of water recalls God's speech to Israel in the book of Ezekiel: "I will sprinkle clean water upon you, and you shall be clean from all your uncleannesses. . . ."

Remember Your Baptism

Our baptism reminds us that it's God's intention to wash us and make us clean, in order that we be effective as a community of servants, testifying to God's power to make all things new. Baptism reflects God's desire that we be reconciled to God and one another. This noble goal is not something we can achieve on our own. Baptism is God's grace poured out in water, testifying to our dependence on what God alone can give.

There is a story that Martin Luther, under attack by his enemies and struggling spiritually, cried out, "I am baptized!" This cry captured his sense that the God who creates the baptismal covenant is, has been, and will be faithful to the end. We can rely upon the promise, however far off we may have drifted: "I will be your God. You will be my people."

In baptizing, the church uses trinitarian language. The minister says, "I baptize you in the name of the Father, and of the Son, and of the Holy Spirit." It is no generic god who lays claim to us, but the God named in scripture—three-in-one, one-in-three. The church has been baptizing into this name since time immemorial. Churches have disputed among themselves about who should be baptized and when and how. Still today, whether at Highland Park Baptist Church, Centenary United Methodist Church, Grace and Holy Trinity Episcopal Church, Second Presbyterian Church, St. Hugo's Roman Catholic Church, or Lima Drive Seventh-Day Adventist Church, baptism is in the name of Father, Son, and Holy Spirit. Whatever the denomination, if baptism is in water and uses these words, Roman Catholics and the historic Protestant churches recognize it as baptism. Since baptism is not into a congregation, or a denomination, or a party, but into the one church of Jesus Christ, it need not be repeated when a person moves from one church to another. It is recognizably the same however much the context may differ.

Today, we are humbled by the recognition that even sacred language may divide. Many of us today are concerned about the use of gender-inclusive language. Yet Father, Son, and Holy Spirit seem not to be gender-inclusive. Some have decided, on their own, to substitute other words for the triune God, such as Creator, Redeemer, and Sustainer. However, these words are not a satisfactory substitute for the traditional language. For one thing, each "person" of the Trinity is Creator, is Redeemer, is Sustainer. The Father is all three; the Son is all three; the Spirit is all three. For another, these three attributes (creating, redeeming, sustaining) are abstractions. They are anonymous. They are impersonal. Nor do they exhibit any relationship between or among three "persons."

We long for reconciliation between male and female, as well as among differing church traditions. Our struggle to manifest our oneness in Christ—woman and man, Catholic and Protestant, Baptist and Presbyterian—requires humility of every one of us. Ever since the story of the Tower of Babel (Genesis 11), language has divided human beings. It can never adequately exhibit the magnificence of the God whose intention is to include us all. Nevertheless, substituting one's own form of words in naming the God into whom we are baptized invites a chaotic situation. It opens the way for even deeper division, in which some churches, in good conscience, have reason to question the baptismal integrity of other churches. And so we persist in the ancient, scriptural, and ecumenical practice, baptizing in the name of the Father, the Son, and the Holy Spirit.

The 30th of March is the anniversary of my baptism, at which my own pastor used those venerable trinitarian words from scripture. My calendar records the baptismal anniversaries of my children, daughters-in-law, and grandchildren. Whenever I have an opportunity, I invite people to look for their baptismal certificates, ask questions of their parents, and discover the date and place and occasion of their own baptisms. Some small annual celebration is certainly in order as we recall the day when the door of the church opened to us, and we became added to God's servant people, whose mission is to be a blessing to "all the families of the earth." Remember your baptism, and be thankful!

5

Heavenly Food: The Lord's Supper

Remembrance

*I*n the film *Places in the Heart*, the final scene takes place in a small country church. Those gathered there belong to a community that has experienced several acts of violence. There are in that church Klansmen, and the African-American man they have lynched, and a sheriff who has been murdered in the line of duty, and people who have loved them or hated them or feared them. The camera follows the action as those assembled pass a tray of cups filled with grape juice from hand to hand. Drawing back, we can see faces. We see faces of those who suffered grievous losses, and those who have inflicted them. We see the faces of those who lost their lives. The dead sit peacefully in the midst of the living, as each receives and hands on the sacred cup.

There is no voice overlaying the soundtrack to explain what is happening. There are no words printed on the screen to clarify this astonishing communion of the living with the dead. The meaning of the scene is in the seeing, rather than the hearing. To many, it will mean nothing, or will prove simply puzzling. To those who have experienced the Sacrament of Holy Communion, it may evoke a sense of intimacy with Christ and one another—an intimacy that leaps over the boundaries that separate people in place and time.

Why do Christians resort to this mini-meal? The tiny bit of bread, the bare sip of wine (or grape juice) are hardly enough to sustain life. Luke tells us that at Jesus' last meal with his disciples, he followed the custom of certain Jewish ceremonial meals, blessing bread and cup. Then, having first given thanks, he gave them to the disciples, saying, "Do this in remembrance of me." Remembering—that's not too hard to understand. Doesn't it have to do with summoning up some past event to savor in the present? Yes, but. I think there's more to remembrance than revisiting the past for present inspiration. Remembrance is not meant only as an effort to energize the memory in order to recover the past or experience for ourselves the impact of past events. Remembrance is rather to hold up Jesus' death and resurrection before the Father, that the Father might remember the gift given. Now, of course, everybody knows that God is not likely to need help from us in jogging the divine memory. The point is not that God may forget cross and empty tomb if we don't issue periodic reminders. The point is that we hold up the memory of Jesus crucified and risen to rejoice *with* God as together those on earth and those in heaven celebrate the divine gift. We are remembering, of course, but we are also celebrating the certainty that God remembers, and that God will be faithful to the promises made and sealed in Jesus' death and resurrection.

From early times, the Great Prayer over the bread and cup at the Communion Table has begun with a dialogue between the presiding minister and the congregation. In that back-and-forth, the minister says, "Let us give thanks to the Lord our God." And the people call out in response, "It is right to give our thanks and praise." The great Communion prayer then moves directly to offering God thanks and praise. For what are we thankful? We are thankful that God remembers and is mindful of Jesus Christ, who represents God's firm commitment to be our God through thick and thin, in life and in death, in this world and in the world to come.

Because the celebration of this sacrament begins with thanks and continues in a great recital of the mighty acts of God for which we are grateful, it was called from early times "Eucharist." Eucharist comes from a Greek word in the Bible that means to give thanks. Protestants are more accustomed to speaking of the Lord's Supper, or Holy Communion. Nevertheless, all sorts of churches—Protestant, Catholic, and Orthodox—appreciate the word Eucharist because it focuses so precisely on the gratitude that energizes our gathering at the Lord's Table. Here we give thanks for God's creation, God's work of liberating the people in bondage, and the sending of God's Word through prophets and others who spoke for God. Most especially, we are thankful for God's gift of Jesus Christ, crucified and risen for us. This Christ breaks down barriers, including those that separate the living from the dead. *Places in the Heart* got it right. Before God we remember, and rejoice, with thanksgiving.

Very often, Protestants associate the Eucharist (or Lord's Supper) exclusively with Jesus' *Last* Supper—the meal he shared with his disciples in an Upper Room on the final night of his life. Because that was a sad and somber occasion, it's hard for us to associate it with thanksgiving. The association of the Lord's Supper with the Last Supper is accurate, to a point. The Eucharist is rooted in actual historical events and centered on one who lived in northern Galilee when it was a Roman province and who finally died a violent death in Judea. The breaking of the bread and the pouring of the cup must recall Jesus' betrayal and death—his body broken on the cross, his life poured out. Inevitably, the Thursday night meal—the Last, agonizing, Supper—comes to mind. Nevertheless, it is too simple to think of the Eucharist as referring only to past events.

The word remembrance tempts us to think of the eucharistic action as an audiovisual exercise to stimulate the memory. In other words, the presumption is that by memory we are supposed to reach back across the centuries to try to connect with a person who once lived but lives no longer. (I wonder if this effort to conjure up the past as though we were there doesn't contribute to the negative experience some Protestants associate with Communion services. Clenching the fists, shutting our eyes tight, and trying to force the memory back, back to Last Supper and Good Friday, is hard work.) The Last Supper and Good Friday are important components of the Eucharist, but for historical reasons we have allowed them to overshadow other dimensions of the Sacrament. The theme of remembrance is likely to throw us off if we think of it only as an internal journey to some past time. Jesus, after all, is alive—not dead.

Holy! Holy! Holy!

In the ancient church and in our church, the minister presiding at the Table invites choirs of angels to join "all the faithful of every time and place" in praise and thanksgiving. Then we sing, "Holy, holy, holy Lord, God of power and might, heaven and earth are full of your glory!"

When we link the Eucharist exclusively with the past, to which we have access only by memory, it can easily become a somber affair. In fact, in both Catholicism and Protestantism, until fairly recently, the death of Jesus has been the most prominent theme. No doubt this has contributed to our uneasiness with having communion frequently. The problem is not that the Eucharist lacks this dimension of suffering and loss, but that when we stop with that, what do we have but a dead Jesus? The early Christians celebrated the Eucharist every Lord's Day. They did so not to fulfill some regulation, or reluctantly, but with anticipation. The anticipation grew out of their conviction that the Lord has risen. In fact, apart from faith in the risen Lord, Eucharists are impossible to sustain. If Jesus is only a martyred prophet, who left us with a body of good advice before his executioners had the last word, then we have nothing to celebrate.

In a congregation I once served, I referred to our worship as celebration. A young man, puzzled at my use of the word, asked, "What are we celebrating?" He was right to ask the question because it's not always evident that we are celebrating anything— or if we are, what that might be. What we are celebrating is that the Lord is risen. We celebrate our confidence that in Jesus' resurrection, God has the last word. Insolent people, defensive religious authorities, uneasy governments, and those who believe that might makes right will not have the last word. Just as Jesus mastered the demonic forces that disfigured people and introduced chaos into the world, God has put down the ultimate destructive power—death itself.

We approach every Eucharistic celebration with the confidence that, by the power of the Holy Spirit, at the Communion Table we shall meet the risen Lord. When the minister presiding calls out to the people, "Lift up your hearts," we lift them up in the hope and expectation of meeting the Christ who died, rose again, and ascended into heaven. When she prays, "Gracious God, pour out your Holy Spirit upon us and upon these your gifts of bread and wine," we trust God to make this whole Table-centered occasion into a time of meeting the living Christ. The Eucharist, then, though rooted in past events, is also a present event. When the minister presiding at the Table says, "Great is the mystery of faith," we burst into song again: "Dying you destroyed our death, rising you restored our life. Lord Jesus, come in glory." Recognizing the presence of the living Christ in our celebrations of Holy Communion, we may decide to carve on our Communion Tables (or embroider on the cloths that grace them) Holy, Holy, Holy! Here, in this place, the Holy One comes to meet us—coming not only out of the past, but coming to us from the future as well. "At the name of Jesus every knee should bend, in heaven and on earth and under the earth, and every tongue should confess that Jesus Christ is Lord, to the glory of God the Father" (Phil. 2:10, 11).

If the Eucharist orients us toward the past, and then toward the present, it also directs us toward the future. Jesus promised his disciples that he would eat and drink with them again "in my Father's kingdom" (Matt. 26:29). Speaking of that ultimate future, Jesus said, "Then people will come from east and west, from north and south, and will eat in the kingdom of God" (Luke 13:29). Some students of the Bible refer to this great ingathering of people at the heavenly table as the Messianic Banquet. (Messiah means Christ.) Of course, it's impossible to speak of heavenly things except in figures of speech. No one can map the streets of heaven, or even begin to describe what life will be like when history has ended, the universe has dissolved, and the whole creation has been transformed. There is no language for it—our speech is entirely inadequate. John Calvin suggested that much of the language and the domestic images of the Bible are like God's baby talk. Baby talk isn't sophisticated, but it's sufficient to get the point across. And so the image of an enormous banquet table in the kingdom of heaven, toward which all sorts of people stream from every direction, is a figure of speech—baby talk. But the point of it is that life in God's kingdom will be at least as delightful as a longed-for family reunion on a lovely summer's day. As the presiding minister reaches the climax of the Great Prayer of Thanksgiving at the Table, all join in praying, "Our Father, who art in heaven, hallowed be thy name, thy kingdom come. . . ."

Every time Christians gather at the Holy Table, the meal is meant to set before us the promise of the Messianic Banquet. Our celebrations are, of course, only a faint shadow of the joy around that heavenly table. Nevertheless, they point us in that direction. The Lord's Supper, then, is at one and the same time about the past, the present, and the future. Holy! Holy! Holy!

A Downpayment on God's Future

At the Lord's Table, it's possible that we may catch a glimpse of the kingdom of heaven. Most of our congregations are made up of people who resemble each other in race and class. In the absence of diversity, it's not so easy to see what the kingdom of heaven might look like. And yet even those congregations where nearly everyone is of the same race and social class have a hidden asset—their children. When the communion elements are taken to the people in the pews, it's easy not to notice the children among us. And yet their visible presence might help to make the inclusiveness of God's kingdom more apparent.

One congregation invites the children to come stand with the presiding minister at the Lord's Table. They have an important role to perform—one that's reminiscent of the role Jewish children play at the Passover Seder. At the Seder, the youngest child asks questions about the meaning of the occasion. For example, "Why is this night different from all other nights?" The host at the Seder table answers, retelling the story of how God liberated the people of Israel from their bondage in the land of Egypt. At the Communion Table in this church, the children also ask questions:

"Why do we give thanks and praise before this Table?" "Why do we eat bread at this Table?" "Why do we drink from the cup at this Table?" "What do we remember at this Table?" In the course of the Great Prayer of Thanksgiving, the presiding minister answers those questions (e.g., "We remember God's gracious love for us, Christ's death and resurrrection for us, and the Spirit's tender care for us.") The children have an important role to play at the very heart of the church's Eucharist. In their role of assisting the presiding minister, they exhibit to some extent the broad welcome of God's Table in that great, heavenly day of reunion and consummation.

After the presiding minister has broken the bread and poured the cup, the congregation come forward to eat and drink, and find places to stand around the Table or near it. The service continues to its conclusion with everyone having left the pews and gathered in a kind of holy chaos as close to the Communion Table as they can get. On a Sunday when there are great numbers of children and youth, plus their parents and older adults, it seems as though in this diversity of ages one can see the kingdom of heaven taking shape before the eyes. This sense of seeing God's ultimate future is even more vivid at denominational gatherings, where those who seek nourishment at the Holy Table are likely to include people of several races and ethnic backgrounds. On such occasions, Jesus' words seem anything but abstract: "Then people will come from east and west, from north and south, and will eat in the kingdom of God" (Luke 13:29).

Is that peaceable kingdom that God has promised as the consummation of history any more than a distant hope? When it takes shape before our eyes, God's future becomes more than just the object of wistful longing. The Eucharist brings God's realm near—so near that we long to see it realized elsewhere in our lives. The moment has not yet arrived when God shall have perfectly healed and reconciled the whole creation. Nevertheless, here and there we witness moments of healing and reconciliation. When we experience a tiny foretaste of it at the Holy Table, we may very well resolve to pray for it and work for it wherever we find ourselves. God's future, brought near in the Lord's Supper, presses on the present. God's ultimate future leaves its mark on our consciousness, makes us discontent with things as they are, whets our appetite for the Messianic banquet, changes us and our expectation of how things ought to be.

One of Jesus' stories helps to unfold the meaning of the Eucharist. He advised his host not to invite to a luncheon or dinner only those who could repay the hospitality. "But when you give a banquet, invite the poor, the crippled, the lame, and the blind" (Luke 14). This, of course, is exactly what God has done through Jesus. God has extended an invitation that includes those who come to the Table absolutely empty-handed. In a sense, that empty-handedness defines every one of us. God has spread the banquet of life before us, and it comes to us entirely as a gift. We did nothing to earn it, nor can we ever even the debt by paying it back in kind. God's Table represents God's astonishing generosity. The biblical term for that extravagant generosity is grace. Grace, exhibited in God's banquet, levels the playing field. Those who accept the hospitality of this Table find that their experience there reframes the world. Caste and clan don't look quite the same to us as they look apart from the Great Banquet.

Promiscuous Dining?

Maybe we're getting a little dreamy-eyed here. How is it possible to put aside the prejudices and anxieties that keep people separated in their less threatening corners? Where in the world can folks find the strength even to consider stretching a hand out across the lines of separation? There is a story in the gospel about Jesus and the disciples and a huge crowd of people at lunchtime (Mark 6). Jesus and the disciples were worn out and thought they would go on retreat. People recognized them, though, and followed them. Pretty soon, a crowd had gathered. They had all wandered out into the country following Jesus, not having given any thought to packing a lunch. The disciples asked Jesus if he wouldn't please send the people away to look for food somewhere in the neighborhood. Jesus didn't like the idea. He said to the disciples, "You give them something to eat."

The disciples knew right away that this was preposterous. They objected, of course. They didn't have the kind of cash it would take to buy food for hordes of people. Jesus didn't argue with them. He asked them to take an inventory of the available supplies. When they calculated that they could find five loaves of bread and two fish, he directed the disciples to order the crowds to sit down on the grass.

Now, here's where the story gets interesting. Mark describes what Jesus did, and Mark's description sounds very much like what the early Christians would have seen at a Sunday service. "Taking the five loaves and the two fish, he looked up to heaven, and *blessed* and *broke* the loaves, and *gave* them to his disciples to set before the people. . . ." Doesn't that sound like a Communion service? The end of the story is that the provisions intended for a small group proved more than enough for the five thousand people sitting on the grass. I think that one point of this story is that the impossible becomes possible when that's what the Lord wants. The disciples had panicked when Jesus had said to them, "You give them something to eat." But he added something to their obedience, and what had been a meager store of supplies somehow became adequate, and there was enough and more.

We may not be very brave or very imaginative in our efforts to care for our stranger-neighbor. But we don't do it by our own strength alone. Every Eucharist, with its taking, blessing, breaking, and giving of bread reminds us of the multiplication of the loaves and fish. The story testifies to God's intention to reduce our anxiety and magnify our meager gifts so that we won't lose heart, and no one need go without.

In New Testament times, people were extremely choosy about whom they invited to dinner, and whose invitations they accepted. To eat with someone implied social and religious compatibility. If you shared a meal with someone whose manner of life was socially unacceptable, you found yourself in a compromised position. Among devout Jews, the arrangement was simple. There were people who were religiously clean, and those who were unclean. You could eat with the former and not with the latter. Jesus repeatedly got into trouble over exactly this issue. The Pharisees, who were among the most devout, criticized him for eating with the wrong people. Jesus accepted the hospitality of tax collectors—those who betrayed their people by acting as agents for the Roman occupying authority. "Why does your teacher eat with tax collectors and sinners?" the Pharisees asked the disciples. The answer Jesus gave was that "those who are well have no need of a physician, but those who are sick" (Matt. 9:12).

At the Communion Table, we come as those who need a physician. And everyone else at the Holy Table comes there on the same terms. Once again, we stand on level ground, each as empty-handed as the other. At the Table we eat and drink grace—pure grace.

The Congregation as Priest

Many churches use a corporate Prayer of Confession in their services. Some object to it, complaining that they are not personally guilty of the sins spelled out in the prayer. It may be that they have, in fact, managed to avoid the specific offenses rehearsed in any given prayer. However, the Prayer of Confession is not the prayer of any individual, but the prayer of the church. Together, we confess the sins of the church—and on behalf of the world, we confess the sins of society, in which we share. Sometimes our sins are not so much offenses we have committed as responsibilities we have evaded. A person might hide away from the hurly-burly of life in society in order to keep his or her hands clean. However, the very act of hiding is offensive to God. Those who seek their own purity by avoiding responsibility fail to hear the gospel that calls us to love and serve our neighbor. We also profit from many of the prejudices and inequalities in society, though we may not be personally responsible for any of them. It is for these reasons that we make a confession of sins whenever we prepare to gather at the Table.

Our Prayer of Confession is a transformation of a prayer used by the officiants at the Roman Catholic Mass. In the pre-Reformation church, the priest prayed the confiteor at the beginning of the Mass. The Protestant Reformers transformed the prayer of those standing at the altar into one actually voiced by the congregation. It is, after all, the congregation that functions as the priest at the Holy Table. The Eucharist is the church's Eucharist—not the Eucharist of ordained priest or minister only. Addressed to the church as a whole, scripture says, "But you are a chosen race, a royal priesthood . . ." (1 Pet. 2:9). The transfer of the prayer of confession from individual priest to the congregation as "royal priesthood" makes a significant statement. It clarifies the fact that it is the church as a whole that celebrates the Lord's Supper—not the ordained person alone. The ordained officer is simply the person appointed to preside at the meal.

The ordained officer is not exercising personal authority when she or he presides at the Table. Ordination is an act by which the church sets aside with prayer and a solemn act of commissioning (the laying on of hands) one whom it empowers to represent Christ in the church in certain ways. The historic Protestant churches ordain their ministers not just for service in particular congregations, nor do they presume that their ministry is limited to a single denomination. Ordination confers the responsibility of serving Jesus Christ in designated roles. The ordained officer exercises her or his ministry, as far as possible, on behalf of the whole Christian church. The church requires an ordained minister to preside at the Table as a sign that the Eucharist belongs to the whole church—and not to individuals, isolated congregations, or even denominations.

The ordained minister—the representative officer—presides on sacramental occasions. Jesus is nevertheless the true host at the Communion Table. (Traditionally, the presiding officer has communed first, as a sign that he or she is not the host, but rather a guest at the table.) But Jesus Christ is not only the host but also the banquet. In the Gospel according to John, Jesus engages in a dialogue with crowds of people who had been present at the feeding of the five thousand. Jesus questions their motivation for coming to look for him. He suspects that their interest in him has been sparked not by a dawning consciousness of who he might be, but simply because he gave them something to eat.

When people in the crowd recall how God gave Israel bread

from heaven to eat when they were wandering in the wilderness, Jesus says, "I tell you, it was not Moses who gave you the bread from heaven, but it is my Father who gives you the true bread from heaven" (John 6:32). This bread "comes down from heaven and gives life to the world." When the crowd asks for some of this bread, Jesus declares, "I am the bread of life." Identifying himself as "the living bread that came down from heaven," Jesus promises, "Whoever eats of this bread will live forever; and the bread that I will give for the life of the world is my flesh" (John 6:51).

This statement throws the crowd into confusion, not surprisingly. When Jesus says, "For my flesh is true food and my blood is true drink," it precipitates a crisis. Certain of those who have followed Jesus "turned back and no longer went about with him" (John 6:66). It may be unlikely that, during his lifetime, Jesus spoke quite so bluntly about his flesh as food and his blood as drink. It's far more likely that this ultragraphic way of speaking demonstrates John's interest in reinforcing what he and the early church believed Jesus represented. He was their feast. It was he who nourished them. It was his whole self (flesh and blood) who fortified them at the Lord's Table. He was host at the Table, and he was the banquet, too.

A Symbol?

Sometimes, in Protestant churches, one hears it said that the Eucharist is only a symbol. The word "only" should never be paired with the word symbol. Someone has suggested a way to test the power of a symbol. Take a photo of a person who's much beloved in the church. Standing before people who appreciate that person, tear up the photo. When you see their reaction, you will know that it's inappropriate to speak of the photograph as "only" a symbol.

Or take, for example, incidents in which someone burns an American flag. The flag is "only" a symbol. Nevertheless, an act of desecration evokes a powerful emotional response. Symbols somehow participate in the reality of what's represented by the symbol. Our Protestant forebears understood this very well and did not speak of the sacraments as "only symbols."

John Knox, a Presbyterian *par excellence,* had this to say about the sacraments in the *Scots Confession* of 1560.

> And so we utterly condemn the vanity of those who affirm the sacraments to be nothing else than naked and bare signs. No, we assuredly believe that by Baptism we are engrafted into Christ Jesus, to be made partakers of his righteousness, by which our sins are covered and remitted, and also that in the Supper rightly used, Christ Jesus is so joined with us that he becomes the very nourishment and food of our souls. *(The Scots Confession)*

Knox did not believe in the Roman Catholic doctrine of transubstantiation—that is, that the bread and wine literally became the body and blood of Christ.

> But this union and conjunction which we have with the body and blood of Christ Jesus . . . is wrought by means of the Holy Ghost, who . . . makes us feed upon the body and blood of Christ Jesus. . . .

It is the Holy Ghost (Holy Spirit) who, we believe, is at work in the whole process of the Eucharistic celebration to deliver Jesus Christ to us, for the nourishing and upbuilding of the church in all its members. It's for this reason that it has been the practice of the church from ancient times to include in the Great Prayer of Thanksgiving at the Holy Table a prayer that the Holy Spirit might "bless and make holy both us and these your gifts of bread and wine, that the bread we break may be a communion in the body of Christ, and the cup we bless may be a communion in the blood of Christ." Just as we offer a Prayer for Illumination, asking the Spirit to deliver Christ to us in scriptures read and the Word preached; and just as we pray for the Holy Spirit to make the waters of baptism "a fountain of deliverance and rebirth"; so do we also pray at the Holy Table that the Spirit might effect what God has promised: to give Jesus Christ to be our spiritual food.

We get in trouble when we try to explain what happens in the

Lord's Supper too precisely. In fact, the Roman Catholic Church's doctrine of transubstantiation is the result of overexplaining. From earliest times, Christians have believed that they meet the risen Christ in the Eucharist. But how does that happen? How is that presence related to the bread and the cup? It's best to leave aside the pretension that this is all explainable.

The historic Protestant churches affirm, as do the Orthodox churches of the East and the Roman Catholic Church, that we do meet Christ in the Supper. The Holy Spirit effects that meeting. To say more than that runs the risk of overreaching. Yet we do not hesitate to say that, at the Table, Jesus Christ truly eats and drinks with us, and becomes our food and drink as well.

Living Presence

Early Protestants borrowed from the prevailing Eucharistic piety of the medieval church an emphasis on the Lord's Supper as primarily a memorial of his death. Right up to our own time, many Protestants continue to think of the Eucharist as a very sober affair. Many think of the Lord's Supper in terms of sitting quietly in a pew, trying hard to visualize the Lord's suffering, while the organ plays funeral hymns softly in the background. However, as noted above, the early Christians experienced the Lord's Supper quite differently. They associated the Lord's Supper not only with Jesus' last meal, but also with pleasant meals before his death, and with post-Resurrection encounters as well.

For example, John's Gospel reports that after Jesus' crucifixion, some of the disciples, at least, went back to their fishing on the Sea of Galilee. Just after daybreak, a figure appeared on the beach. John tells the reader that the figure was Jesus—but the disciples didn't know that at first. When they did recognize him, they raced back to shore as fast as they could. They found that Jesus had started a charcoal fire and was broiling fish for their breakfast. John says that "Jesus came and took the bread and gave it to them, and did the same with the fish" (John 21:13). The gestures of taking and giving signal that John and the church understood this to be a Eucharistic action.

The story of the disciples who met the risen Jesus on the road to Emmaus (noted above) is similar. Jesus, as yet unrecognized, "*took* bread, *blessed* and *broke* it, and *gave* it to them." The two disciples had hurried back to Jerusalem to report their eye-opening experience to the eleven disciples. "Then they told what had happened on the road, and how he had been made known to them in the breaking of the bread" (Luke 24:35).

The post-Resurrection meals shaped the expectations the early Christians brought to the Eucharist. They expected not only to reflect on the Lord's death but also to rejoice in his living presence. In the twentieth century, many churches—both Catholic and Protestant—have restructured their guidelines for Holy Communion and rewritten the texts of their Communion services. They have done so in the light of more recent scholarship that has drawn attention to the central role of the risen Christ in the early Eucharistic practice of the church. Presbyterian, Methodist, Episcopal, Lutheran, and other churches have shifted the accent of their Communion celebrations from funereal to joyful. There is no intention to deny the role of Christ's suffering on the cross, but his death cannot be isolated from his resurrection.

Churches that have adapted to this change of accent may make use of color, movement, congregational song, and other kinds of music associated with Easter rather than Good Friday. When congregations rediscover the Eucharist as a joyful reunion with the living Christ and all the baptized (living and dead), the Lord's Supper becomes an event to be welcomed and enjoyed frequently, rather than "observed" occasionally.

Variations in Tone

Of course, the emotional tenor of the Communion service will vary, just as ordinary meals do. At Thanksgiving, Christmas, and New Year's, our family meals are festive and upbeat. Meals that accompany a death in the family, or a farewell to one who is leaving home or moving away, will have an underlying tone of wistfulness—as well as offering opportunity for storytelling about events in the past. The Communion service on Maundy Thursday will be different in emotional complexion from the Communion service on Pentecost—and both will be different from the one on Christmas eve. But in every gathering at the Lord's Table, just as in nearly every ordinary meal, there will be a mixture of sobriety and lightheartedness. There is awareness of loss—of sacrifice—and of immeasurable gain. The Eucharist recalls how, in cross and empty tomb, the Lord demonstrated the truth of his own words: "Those who lose their life for my sake will find it" (Matt. 10:39b).

We are baptized only once. Baptism is the sealing of the covenant between God and church: "I will be your God, you will be my people." The Lord's Supper is the covenant meal between God and people. Every time we share it, each party reaffirms the baptismal covenant. By its very nature, the Lord's Supper is the meal of the community, the church. It is not to be celebrated or consumed all alone. In it, we affirm the covenant bond that links us with the risen Lord and all the baptized, living or dead. As in the film *Places in the Heart*, the Holy Table is the gathering place for brothers and sisters visibly and tangibly present, and for sisters and brothers present but not visible to the eye. Together with "angels and archangels and all the company of heaven," we praise God for mighty acts, recall with thanks God's work of redemption, call upon the Holy Spirit, and offer our praise to the Triune God: Father, Son, and Holy Spirit. Thus ends the Great Prayer of Thanksgiving: "Through Christ, with Christ, in Christ, in the unity of the Holy Spirit, all glory and honor are yours, almighty Father, now and forever."

6

Sacrament: Am I Missing Something Here?

Something Missing?

A few years ago, I traveled to Israel with a group of students and one of their professors from a nearby seminary. Before we set out, one of my colleagues asked me to bring her back a bottle of water from the Jordan River. It seemed a harmless request, and I nearly forgot about it until we actually found ourselves on the banks of the Jordan, near the city of Tiberias. We weren't alone there. A number of other pilgrims shared the site with us. Among them was a group of women, all dressed more or less alike in long black dresses. We guessed that they might be Orthodox women from Cyprus. They had shyly tiptoed into the water, then lost all their inhibitions. They merrily splashed each other and themselves, laughing and singing all the while. We watched curiously from the bank, not tempted to join them.

All at once remembering my colleague's request, I rummaged in my shoulder bag and found a nearly empty bottle of commercially bottled water. Emptying it, I made my way to the edge of the river and filled the bottle with water from the Jordan. A young woman from our group, soon to graduate from the seminary, watched me. Her gaze made me self-conscious. As I arose, somewhat sheepishly, she inquired, "Am I missing something here?"

I was embarrassed. I had been caught behaving like one of the Orthodox women exulting in the holy waters of this sacred place. Unlike them, I was thoroughly immersed in a secular society, and in the culture of a Protestant church that was wary of the dangers of idolatry. We knew, didn't we, that there is no such thing as a holy place or a holy substance. All water is the same, from God's point of view. The water in my bottle, as a matter of fact, had flowed from the Sea of Galilee that very day, and, not long before that, had descended from the heights of Mt. Hermon. Its history was no older than last winter's snow. Jesus had no more to do with that water than with the water of the Ohio River. And the place where the women cavorted in the water was a place constructed for tourists. It's not at all likely that this was the spot where John the Baptist had baptized.

The young woman's question, "Am I missing something here?" brought me up short. It was as though I had been caught in some superstitious act—something we might tolerate among simple people, like the women in black, but scorn among the enlightened. I'm sure that my face reddened. I muttered something noncommittal. "Not that I know of." End of conversation. Slinking away, I hid my bottle of water in my shoulder bag.

Later, as you might imagine, I pondered what had happened that morning on the bank of the Jordan. Why had I been moved to gather that water? What did it mean that the young woman was so disdainful? And most of all, could I have come up with a better response to her "Am I missing something here?" than a defensive "Not that I know of"? The more I thought about it, the more it seemed to me that I had no need to be either embarrassed or apologetic. My response might better have been "Yes, you may be missing something here."

I had known that the water of the Jordan was not holy. It had no power to sanctify, or cure, or protect. And yet that water, fresh from Mt. Hermon via the Sea of Galilee, created the same river that had flowed in that place for thousands of years. The people of Israel had crossed it when they ended their forty-year journey in the wilderness, having been liberated from their generations of bondage in Egypt. John the Baptist had conducted his ministry at the edge of that river. And Jesus had come out to see and hear John; had stood in line with everyday sinners to be baptized in that river.

The water I gathered in my plastic bottle had no magic or

supernatural powers, but it did have the power to awaken associations. It had the power to evoke memory, and to reduce the sense of distance between my own life and the sacred history associated with this stream. It played a similar role to that of the photos I keep in my wallet. When I'm separated from my family, I look at their pictures and somehow their reality touches me more deeply than when I simply try to imagine them in my mind's eye. And yet I would never mistake the photo for the person.

I suspect that, similarly, every time my colleague glanced at the bottle of Jordan River water sitting on her bookshelf, she would, for a moment, feel herself nearer to Jesus, who had heard at his baptism God's voice confirming his identity and mission. This would say something to her about her own calling and her own mission. And if one day it no longer did that, she could pour the water down the sink without giving it a second thought.

The Sacred in the Ordinary

The same group of seminary students with whom I traveled had also visited the Garden Tomb in Jerusalem. While most scholars agree that the Garden Tomb is probably not the actual site of Jesus' burial and his resurrection appearances, it looks very much like what that place must have looked like. It's far easier to imagine the first Easter there than at the Church of the Holy Sepulcher in Jerusalem, the more likely site of the original tomb. At the Garden Tomb there are also many groups of pilgrims. They have to take turns, each group waiting until the preceding group has paid its visit before moving in for a closer examination. Our group watched from a distance while a group of Korean pilgrims approached the tomb, singing hymns and praying. The demeanor of our group resembled that of adolescent skeptics. Poking each other, the students shared their amusement at what they seemed to regard as the naive piety of the Koreans. The underlying message, shared wordlessly among the seminarians, but clear enough from their stifled laughter, was that the Garden Tomb was a fraud—but even if it had been authentic, it's just rocks and a hole after all. It is not—and could not be—any more sacred than any other place.

The students' discomfort with the danger of showing reverence for a sacred site is rooted, at least in part, in the Protestant loathing of idolatry. One can see the danger of idolatry in the Old City of Jerusalem, where various Catholic and Orthodox jurisdictions have quarreled shamelessly over space in the Church of the Holy Sepulcher. A healthy dose of Protestant skepticism might be just what the feuding parties need. And yet it may also be that the students' amusement at the Koreans' piety at the Garden Tomb is another case of missing something. Of course, both the Garden Tomb and the traditional tomb in the Church of the Holy Sepulcher are nothing but rocks and a hole. Nevertheless, each evokes associations with Jesus Christ crucified, buried, and risen. Is there someplace in between rank superstition and patronizing scorn?

It's easy, sometimes, to mistake Christianity for just another kind of good advice—wise suggestions about how to live a healthy life in harmony with God and one's neighbors. Certainly it is a kind of wisdom that may guide our lives, but it's more than that. The Christian faith testifies to a people's conviction that God has visited our planet as a human being. That human being is Jesus of Nazareth. Although he was certainly human, as we are, he also bore the person and presence of God into our space and time. There is a doctrine that names that conviction. In the church, we speak of the doctrine of the Incarnation. The word *incarnation* comes from Latin roots. In English, we have the words carnal and carnivorous. The word *carnal* refers to temptations of the flesh, and a carnivore is an animal that eats flesh. Incarnation is another English word derived from the same Latin root. It means that God became flesh—a human being. The Bible does not use the word *incarnation,* but John points to it in his Gospel when he says, "In the beginning was the Word, and the Word was with God, and the Word was God. . . . And the Word became flesh and lived among us, and we have seen his glory . . ." (John 1:1,14).

Christians believe that because God has become flesh—that is, become incarnate in Jesus of Nazareth—God has hallowed all flesh. God has not disdained the physical world, nor despised the human body. God's person and power need not operate only far above our heads, invisibly, in some immaterial sphere far removed from the nitty-gritty of human life. In fact, God's presence has been displayed in a fully human being. We must not imagine Jesus of Nazareth as walking two or three feet above the ground, as though he were a purely spiritual being, too spiritual to risk contamination from the earth. The God who made a home along-side us in Mary's son has blessed the created world and made it clear that ordinary and physical things can be bearers of the most sacred reality.

The Incarnation Hallows the Material World

From even before the beginnings of the Christian community, John the Baptist baptized people in water. Christians also baptized, and because of their experience with Jesus, they saw in baptism dimensions of meaning beyond what John had been able to see. Jesus shared a good many meals with his disciples and, at the last meal he ate with them, graphically related the breaking of a loaf and the pouring of a cup to his impending martyrdom. Like the bread and cup, his body would soon be broken, and his life poured out. Jesus directed his disciples to continue eating a meal of bread and wine "in remembrance of me." In acts of healing, Jesus had from time to time made use of spittle and mud. Mark tells us that when Jesus sent the twelve disciples out in pairs on a mission, "they . . . anointed with oil many who were sick, and cured them." From very early on, the church made use of these ordinary, physical things without feeling as though their use somehow betrayed a genuinely Christian spirituality. They used water, bread, wine, and oil without apology or embarrassment, in the expectation that the God who had become incarnate in Christ could continue to wash, nourish, and heal. Of course, God can wash, nourish, and heal without the use of any material substances at all. And the use of material substances cannot bind God, somehow requiring God to show up and perform. On the other hand, in Christ God has bent down to us human beings in our weakness, using physical things to make God's Word and power tangible and accessible. God has made accommodation for us who live in a material world since we must meet God within it, not having access to God outside it.

Near the middle of the last century, some New England Congregationalists reached the conclusion that the Christianity they had received didn't square with modern knowledge. Ralph Waldo Emerson, among others, became a Unitarian minister. As his thought developed, he decided that he could no longer, in good conscience, preside at the Lord's Supper. He believed that he and others had outgrown the use of this sacrament. Although it may have suited the people of the Middle East, where it originated, it was foreign to Emerson and offended his sensibilities. He suggested to the officers of his church that they substitute a service of his design, not including bread and cup.

Emerson's view of Jesus was primarily as a teacher who had come to enlighten human beings with certain universal principles. His death on the cross was sad, but irrelevant to his mission, except that prophets frequently experience rejection. I'm not sure what Emerson made of Jesus' resurrection, but I suspect that he took it as a symbol representing the eventual triumph of good over evil. Given his theology, it's not at all surprising that Emerson developed a distaste for the sacrament of Jesus' body and blood. What Jesus offered was not himself—but teachings, ideas, principles.

The fact that the historic churches make use of water, bread, and the fruit of the vine is not just a quaint custom, somewhat primitive in nature, which has managed to survive even in these enlightened times. Our use of these material things is a statement about our core belief. At the very heart of the faith of the historic churches is belief that God has become incarnate in Christ. What God gives us in Christ is not simply a set of principles to live by, but Christ's own self. Nor was Christ simply a spirit who *seemed* to be a flesh-and-blood human being. Christ shares every aspect of our human nature, including its straightforward physicality. Our practice of baptism (with real water) and Eucharist (with real bread and the fruit of the vine) testifies to the church's conviction about who Christ is, the reality of his ministry among us, and his true suffering, death, burial, and resurrection *for us*. Although the old Protestant wariness of idolatry must always serve as a caution, nevertheless, as those whose faith is an incarnational faith, we cannot deny that physical things may serve God's purposes. Can bread and wine represent the Christ who is God's gift to the world? They can. Is it okay to collect a plastic bottle of water from the Jordan River? Sure, why not? No harm done, as long as I don't drink it in place of asking the doctor for a prescription for antibiotics; or pour it over a hospital patient in the expectation of a miraculous cure; or bow down and pray to it as though it could stand in for Jesus Christ.

Old Quarrels

There is a difference, of course, in the way Roman Catholics have used physical things and the way Protestants have. Roman Catholics have traditionally valued relics of particularly notable or holy people (saints). In their altars one may find the knucklebone of a martyr or a hank of hair from an extraordinary servant of the church, or even a fragment of the true cross. In medieval times, this reverence for relics of saints commanded far more serious respect than it does in North American or European Catholicism today. Until Vatican II, Roman Catholics also felt little restraint in creating statues to represent holy people—including not only saints but also, of course, Mary and Joseph, and certainly Jesus himself as infant, child, or grown man. The apparent lack of restraint with which Roman Catholics filled their churches with such images on the eve of the Reformation contributed to their wholesale rejection by Protestants. The mission of the Protestant Reformation was to get back to essentials. To do that might very well require the paring away of all sorts of elaborations that had crowded their way into church life, stealing attention from Jesus Christ, who is the very center of Christian faith. On the eve of the Reformation, most churches included not only stained glass and paintings on the walls, but often many side altars decorated with representations of Jesus, the Holy Family, and various saints. People praying at these altars might fix their gaze on one of these images and, it seemed, even direct their prayers toward them. Holy parades, in which the devout carried a statue of the Blessed Virgin through the streets, were common. They displayed or paraded holy relics. Priests and their attendants exposed the Blessed Sacrament itself (the consecrated bread) in outdoor processions, while those who saw it knelt and made the sign of the cross. Those drawn to Protestantism considered all of this to be superstitious, perilously close to idolatry.

Some Protestants, reading Jesus' statement in John's Gospel that "God is spirit, and those who worship him must worship in spirit and in truth" (John 4:24), jumped to the conclusion that spirit and truth meant with words only. This was particularly true of Protestants removed by a generation or two from the Reformation period. While Baptism and the Lord's Supper were too clearly authenticated in scripture to be laid aside, they were decidedly less important than preaching, praying, and singing. After all, the words of the preacher are invisible—spiritual?—as prayers and hymns are. (What fell upon the ear must have seemed less prone to idolatry than what fell upon the eye or tongue.) In reacting against one extreme, Protestants moved toward another. In their case, they ran the risk of spiritualizing—and, finally, denying—the reality of the Incarnation on which all genuine Christian faith rests.

We are the heirs of some of these historic overcorrections. We are not as uneasy with stained glass windows, other visual arts (e.g., banners), candles, crosses, and other symbols as some of our Protestant forebears were. Nevertheless, we have definitely favored forms of worship that lean heavily on words (said or sung). As we have seen, it was pure historical circumstance—not Protestant principle—that led to the reduction of the meal to an occasional affair, though, from the beginning, it had been meant to be the climax of every Sunday service. That diminishment of the Sacrament has been reinforced by a suspicion of the material world, as though material and spiritual were in conflict. To the extent that we have identified spirit with words only, and become uneasy with water, bread, and wine, we have drifted away from our anchorage in the doctrine of the Incarnation.

It's Not 1517 Any More

Are we Protestants still reacting to the excesses of the medieval Catholic church? Guess what! It's not 1517 any more! The medieval Catholic church as such no longer exists. Although Protestants will still encounter species of Catholic piety that make us squeamish, they are likely to make official Roman Catholicism squeamish, too. Today our Protestant protest is primarily a positive affirmation of the biblical faith in all its richness. And if we are protesting *against* anything, it would be indifference, lack of faith, and unthinking, superficial, and indiscriminate forms of religiosity. We are not Roman Catholics, but neither are we locked in battle with them. The world, as always, is full of bewildered people who need something to believe in. Idols of various sorts may serve the purpose for a while, but false gods always let us down in the end. It is the responsibility of Christians—Protestant, Catholic, Orthodox—to testify to the God not made by human hands, nor merely a product of the human imagination. This God—whom we worship as Father, Son, and Holy Spirit—will not let us down.

The question is, How shall we represent this God, who is bigger than every word, symbol, or gesture we might employ to speak of God? Someone has said, "Preach the gospel every day. If necessary, use words." The church preaches the gospel when it builds a house for a poor family, collects food for the hungry, provides a homeless shelter or soup kitchen, paints a house in Appalachia, provides a day care center or, sticks up for people who can't make their voices heard where it counts.

One hundred and fifty years ago, nearly every good thing that was done was done by the churches, or at least done in the name of Christ. But these days, there are lots of persons and agencies doing good deeds, motivated by a variety of humanitarian reasons. Without words, we ourselves may not understand that the good we are called to do we are in fact *called* to do. We need to use words. In a society where there is so much spiritual barrenness, words are essential.

But are words enough? God has graciously provided us with other means to testify to God's reality: certain uses of water, bread, and wine. There have been physical gestures used by Christians since the time of Jesus: human touch—the laying on of hands to pray for or commission someone and anointing with oil as a kind of enacted prayer for the sick. "Are any among you sick? They should call for the elders of the church and have them pray over them, anointing them with oil in the name of the Lord" (James 5:14).

In a time when artists, architects, the designers of web pages, filmmakers, interior designers, and gourmet cooks appeal to the eye, does it make sense for Christians to leave behind or diminish the large visible actions of washing with water, breaking bread, pouring the cup? In an age in which bottling the right scent can make people rich, does it make sense for the church to sacrifice the evocative aroma of bread and wine? Or the fragrant scent of oil for anointing? In an age when many live in physical and even emotional isolation among the urban masses, does it make sense for the church to forget the power of the benign touch—the laying on of hands?

An Outward and Visible Sign . . .

This may be the place to look more closely at the word *sacrament*. The word doesn't appear in the Bible. The word has been understood in various ways, but it's easy to see in it a similarity to the word *sacred*. St. Augustine and others have described a sacrament as "an outward and visible sign of an inward and spiritual grace." Roman Catholics have used the word *sacrament* to describe seven rites of the church: baptism, confirmation, penance (confession), Eucharist, ordination, marriage, and anointing of the sick. Protestants have insisted that it's proper to use the word only in reference to two of those rites, baptism and the Lord's Supper (Eucharist). Justification for limiting the term *sacrament* to these two has been that it was only these two actions that the Lord himself instituted, and only these two that in symbolic ways represent his death and resurrection. However, this dispute over what is a sacrament is in a way a futile one, since there is no evidence that Jesus intended to create a category by which to classify certain rites or actions. It would seem, then, that the church is free to use the term somewhat flexibly, insofar as a general term is useful. For example, out of their own experience, Protestants would argue that preaching is sacramental, though not, properly speaking, one of the two (or seven) sacraments.

What do we mean when we speak of something as sacramental? Something is sacramental when it becomes a means by which Jesus Christ in his life, death, and resurrection becomes manifest to his people. A material thing—whether it be water, bread, wine, the printed words of scripture, or the vibration of a human voice on the ear—becomes sacramental when Christ uses it to open us to his presence.

In preaching, for example, the preacher's task is to employ her or his scholarship, skill, imagination, personality, and voice as a vessel by which Christ may become present to his community. The preacher's words are merely human words. Nevertheless, by the power of the Holy Spirit, they may become God's Word to those who listen for it. Through, in, under (and often in spite of) the preacher's human creation—the sermon—the Spirit delivers to the people the presence and power of Jesus Christ.

By means of this very human vehicle, Christ stands among God's people to comfort, warn, teach, challenge, call, charge with a mission, console, judge, arouse, strengthen, assure, and simply be present to them. The work of the sermon, then, is not to satisfy the preacher's need to do any one of those things. The one who preaches crafts the sermon with the prayer that the Christ exhibited in the scriptures may step into the congregation's presence to say and do whatever he wants to say and do.

Reading scripture may also be described as sacramental. Scripture cannot be reduced to a single category. It's not a moral handbook, a manual of laws, a theological textbook, inspirational poetry, clever case studies, history, reminiscences, or a collection of hymns, creeds, or doctrines. And yet within scripture the reader finds traces of all those things and more, often so mixed together that it's hard to distinguish one from the other. Particularly when read in concert with others, the words and patterns of scripture become transparent, so to speak. We look at them, but also through them, to see what God is disclosing to us. We listen to them and hear ordinary human words, sometimes reflecting the particular spin of another place and time; but we may also hear a Word from the Lord.

In fact, the church through the centuries has over and over again heard in scripture a Word from the Lord that has repeatedly called people to faith and sustained them in service. Scripture and preaching are and must always be closely bound together. They are certainly bound together in this one thing—each is sacramental. Each, though marked with every sign of humanity, may become a means by which the Lord claims the attention of God's people. Note the use of the word "may." It's not inevitable. It's possible to read the Bible and understand its words and follow the flow of its thought and hear no Word from the Lord—or hear a distorted word, which echoes one's own biases. It's possible to hear preaching and hear no Word from the Lord—only a multiplication of syllables.

Our Protestant forebears believed that it was only by the power of the Holy Spirit that words—biblical words or the words of preachers—might become for us the Word of God. Human beings simply don't have the capacity to tune in to God without God's own help. There are too many messages in our environment, and our self-interest is so great, that by ourselves we cannot distinguish God's Word from some other word. Apart from the Spirit, the words of the Bible or the words of the preacher are just words. Maybe they attract our interest, maybe they simply bore us—but they don't penetrate our defenses. For that reason, our Protestant forebears always prayed for the illumination of the Spirit before reading scripture aloud in church—a reading that led to and shaped the sermon to be preached.

Signs of Jesus' Death and Resurrection

The two rites that Protestants call sacraments resemble the reading of scripture and preaching in certain respects. While scripture and sermon use human thoughts and words, baptism and

Eucharist use water, bread, and the fruit of the vine. In baptism and the Lord's Supper, there are also human voices and gestures. Through, in, and under water, bread, wine, voice, and gesture, Jesus Christ crucified and risen draws near to those who trust him. The water, to be sure, is nothing but water. And yet in this simple rite of cleansing, drowning, and birthing, people of faith may discern Christ in his death and resurrection. The bread and wine are identical to bread and wine consumed in one's own home. And yet, in the rite of blessing, breaking, pouring, and sharing, we discern Christ's death and his life poured out, only to become spiritual nourishment for those who receive this gift in faith. These material things become channels for God's grace—means by which the risen Christ gathers us to himself.

If we look upon these ordinary things through the lenses of faith, we may see and meet the Christ who joins his people in the cross-shaped places of this world, and lifts us, with him, into his resurrection life. Our forebears in the faith understood that, apart from the Holy Spirit, people will see nothing but water, and nothing but an ordinary loaf and cup. So it is that, just as we pray for the Spirit's illumination before reading scripture and preaching, we also pray for the Holy Spirit to bring Christ near in water, bread, and cup.

The Spirit doesn't change the water into something else, or the bread and wine into something else. The elements remain what they were, but the Spirit transforms us so that in them we see and experience the Christ who has promised to be with us in these actions.

There have been some who describe the church itself as a kind of sacrament. Most often we look at the church and we see something very human. The church is, in some respects, an institution like any other. Sociologists can study it, map its demographics, chart the behaviors of its members and describe their most common habits of thought, and to some extent measure its impact—positive or negative—on society. Historians can document its development, diagram the outlines of its inner disputes, and record its sins. All of this observation and study demonstrates the obvious—the church is made up of human beings and bears the mark of their virtues and of their every weakness.

However, there's another way of looking at the church, too. Those who look at the church with the eyes of faith will see there some sign of the life, dying, and rising of its Lord. Some, in faith, will see in this human institution the marks of the cross and the promise of the resurrection. If the Spirit gives insight, some will see the church as a human vessel from which one may drink the wine of God's new creation. In that sense, the church itself is sacramental—a visible entity that becomes a channel revealing the graciousness and love of God.

More Than Meets the Eye

It may be that a stranger will come into your church next Sunday morning. She or he will hear a reading from the Bible and try to follow the sermon. There will be a baptism and the Lord's Supper. The stranger may find some of these things more or less familiar. The reading of scripture resembles other kinds of readings the stranger may have heard. The sermon is not entirely unlike other forms of public speaking. And yet the stranger may nevertheless find herself bewildered. Maybe she will be too polite to ask, "Am I missing something here?" The minister will baptize, perhaps, two children and an adult. The stranger, observing this strange rite without any previous introduction, may ask, "Am I missing something here?" Watching attentively the blessing of bread and cup, and the sharing from hand to hand, the question may surface again: "Am I missing something here?" The answer, of course, in each case, is "Yes. You may be missing something here." There is, after all, more here than meets the eye.

It may not be a stranger who's puzzled by Word or Sacrament. It may be the longtime church member for whom none of this has ever clicked. The words, the gestures, the basic materials are familiar, but they remain disconnected, forming no clear picture. This one, too, may be wondering quietly, if not out loud, "Am I missing something here?"

It's not surprising that someone should experience a certain bewilderment in the presence of these actions. These are strange things that we do. They're somewhat familiar, of course, to most people in Western society after two thousand years. If people have had no direct exposure to Bible, preaching, or sacraments, they have usually had some introduction to them in the art and literature of the West. Nevertheless, familiar or not, they are strange. If, by their very strangeness, they arouse enough curiosity for either secular or religious people to ask, "Am I missing something here?" it will be a good thing. What we do in worship is and ought to be different enough from other assemblies that it provokes that very question. Once a person has raised that question, she or he has already become open, even if only just a little bit, to the possible reply "You may indeed be missing something. What do you suppose it might be?"

The Eastern Orthodox churches have used the word *mysteries* where the Western churches have used *sacraments*. There may be wisdom in that choice of words. A mystery, as used in this way, doesn't refer to something that doesn't make sense. Rather, it refers to something that makes more sense than we can put into words. In this age of anxiety in the historic churches, the great temptation is to panic. We look at the churches that claim the largest numbers and face great temptation to imitate them, impulsively gambling on the possibility that we may get the same statistical results that they have. We invest in technology, put the denominational name in small print, try to think how to make the sermon (by some other name) entertaining, and introduce music we don't understand ourselves. We bet the farm on the possibility of numerical success, so desperate that we don't think about what we will become should we succeed.

It seems as though the last thing we Christians have learned to resort to is something that God has provided for us from the very beginning of the church. In times of transition, we have a wonderful opportunity to bring out old treasures that are still new. Before we bet everything on the latest poll, let's first consider the value of bringing forward what's inadvertently been left at the edges—the treasures hidden away in the church's storehouse—the sacraments, rooted in the Lord's own Word—Christ's life, death, and resurrection.

7

Where Are We Headed?

Catholics and Protestants:
Reviewing the Situation

Occasionally, I hear grumbling from someone in the pew: "Why are we getting to be so much like the Catholics?" Over at Our Lady Queen of Martyrs, the pastor has heard complaints for the past thirty years: "Why are we getting to be so much like the Protestants?" The fact is that there have been significant changes in the worship practices of most mainline Protestant churches in the past few decades. There have also been notable changes in Roman Catholic worship during the same period. Are the Protestants imitating the Catholics? Or are the Catholics trying to mimic the Protestants?

The fact is that neither is trying to copy the other. In the twentieth century, several forces have combined to direct the attention of both Protestants and Catholics to questions of worship. Catholics and Protestants alike have turned to the same sources to explore those questions. They have looked, first of all, to the Bible. The past century witnessed an enormous growth in interest in the scriptures and a vast body of biblical scholarship. It may seem to the casual reader that the Bible has very little to say about worship. It's true, certainly, that the scripture is not a manual that prescribes particular orders or styles of worship. Nevertheless, when one approaches the Bible with an interest in questions of worship, it yields an astonishing amount of information.

Catholics read the biblical scholarship written by Protestants, and vice versa. What each has discovered is that the norm for Christian worship is Word *and* Sacrament—Sacrament *and* Word.

Protestants and Catholics have also turned to the history of the development of Christian worship. Each has reread materials from the first centuries of the church, to discover the development of worship practices and the reasons that seem to underlie that development. Both groups have examined the worship of the medieval church on the eve of the Reformation. They have studied the controversies about worship that emerged during the Reformation period. Historical study shows how the Word became eclipsed in the Catholic church, and the Sacrament pushed to the edges in the Protestant churches. Both Protestants and Catholics have concluded that their own worship practices—however much cherished—are, in some respects, deficient. Each has fallen short of the ideal. Many Catholics have felt the need to recover a strong tradition of preaching the gospel, and many Protestants have felt the urgency of rediscovering the power and place of the Sacrament.

It is true, then, that in the course of decades, Protestant worship has come to resemble Catholic worship, and Catholic worship has come to resemble Protestant worship. Neither is deliberately imitating the other, but both have reached similar conclusions based on their biblical and historical study. It's cause for celebration that Protestants and Catholics have come to the point where they can reach similar conclusions without scaring themselves silly. The time is past when Catholic and Protestant identify each other as opponents to be countered at all costs. It's clear to both communities that it is no longer profitable to shape their worship practices by trying to be as different as possible each from the other. What sense does it make for either to pattern their worship practices on the presumption that whatever one group does, the other must abhor? We live in a different era.

Shifting Alliances

Someone has suggested that there are two kinds of people: those who divide the world into two kinds of people and those who don't. Of course, it's too simple ever to divide the human race into two kinds. But if we were to play that game, North America could not reasonably be divided into Protestant and Catholic. More likely, we might see the world as divided between religious and secular—or Christian and non-Christian. In any case, however we as Christians might choose to draw the distinctions, Catholics and mainline Protestants in turn-of-the-century North America find themselves on the same team. Of course, differences remain. Nevertheless, in spite of our history of conflict, we stand together as Christians in a world grown increasingly secular, on the one hand—and, on the other, increasingly religious in ways distant from Christianity. We also stand together as historic bodies that take seriously the deep tradition of the church, while recoiling from the various fundamentalisms so popular these days.

The past century is one in which it's clear that large numbers of people who might once have identified themselves as Christian now see themselves as separated from the church and its faith. This became particularly evident in Europe in the opening decades of the twentieth century. Protestant and Catholic alike began to ask why the working classes seemed alienated from the church. A story is told about two factory workers in France, crossing the same square they had crossed every day for twenty years. In the square there stood a crucifix—the body of Jesus on the cross. One of the workmen interrupted their casual conversation. He poked the other and asked, "Say, who is that fellow there?"

In France and Scotland, as well as other countries, priests and ministers in the mid-twentieth century looked for ways to reclaim the laboring classes. One of the first issues that arose was that of worship. They asked themselves whether the worship of their churches had somehow become elitist—inaccessible to the experience of working folk. A desire to reconnect with this huge population motivated a good deal of interest in worship among both Protestants and Catholics.

One example of the intersection between a desire to relate to working people and to renew the worship life of the church is the Iona community in Scotland. The Iona community had its origins in the slums of Glasgow. A group of ministers and laypeople in the Church of Scotland felt drawn to ministry with the working classes. It became part of their agenda to reinvigorate their inherited tradition of worship. They were not motivated simply by antiquarian interests or historical curiosity of an academic kind. They knew that in worship there is power, and they looked to the sources to see if they could find worship practices that had been means of empowerment to other generations of Christians. What they found was that there is power in worship in which Word and Sacrament come together. Their reflection led them to the conviction that the best worship cannot be worship contained entirely in the head. The best worship engages the whole self. Fully Christian worship must bring the Sacrament alongside the Word. The Iona community, developing its unique ministry both in Glasgow and on the island of Iona, has led in the effort to renew worship in the Church of Scotland. A good many Americans, drawn to their interests and values, spent time with the Iona community—some becoming permanent members though living abroad. When they came back to the United States, some of them became leaders in movements dedicated to the renewal of worship in American churches. Many of the changes in Protestant worship practices since the 1950s can be traced to their influence.

Getting the Picture

What became evident in Europe early in the twentieth century became obvious in North America only later in the century. Whereas once it could be nearly taken for granted that any American who wasn't Jewish was either Protestant or (somewhat less likely) Catholic, nothing at all can be taken for granted anymore. The 1960s saw a surge of interest in Eastern religions, or in short-cut versions of Eastern religions. There are growing communities of Buddhists, Muslims, and Hindus in North America—mostly immigrants, but with significant numbers of native-born members. Society no longer presumes that a person must have a religious identity. Many raised in churches cast off that relation when they become adults. Others practice spiritual disciplines of an astonishing variety—most quite distant from either Judaism or Christianity. What thoughtful European Christians began to notice many years ago, American Christians have recently begun to recognize: we no longer live in a society in which Christianity—much less Protestantism—is the default setting.

It's probably true that every generation introduces some sort of new crisis for the church. Over the centuries there have been many such crises. Sometimes the church has met those crises in a timely fashion. Other times, it has been way too late responding to the challenges posed by new developments. North American Protestants for so long occupied the position of a kind of informal religious establishment that it has taken awhile for them to recognize that there have been far-reaching changes in their status. The reasons for that change are complex. Perhaps much of the change can be traced to the social phenomena of the 1960s, in which a whole generation became suspicious of institutions and authority of any kind—including religious institutions and authority. It was an era of revolt—particularly against racial injustice and the war in Vietnam, perceived as misguided and unjust. The ethos of rebellion kindled a disdain for the systems of faith and morality long held in respect in American society. Presumably, those systems had helped to create the unfortunate *status quo*, and blessed the powers that seemed to be leading the nation to ruin. Certainly from that decade forward, Protestant churches have not been able to take for granted the continuing loyalty of even the children of their own members.

Three decades later, Protestants have at last begun to get the picture. At least, most of their leadership has. In some ways, the mainline churches have moved from semi-establishment status to something like a cultural minority. The churches experience this change in status as a crisis. Not to say that crises are necessarily bad. In fact, they may create wonderful new opportunities. Nevertheless, like other crises in the history of the church, this one shakes our complacency and requires us to reassess almost everything about our church life—including our worship.

There were, of course, some people who spotted the crisis—and the challenge—sooner than others. They realized that younger generations were staying away from the churches in droves. Compelled by a desire to reach those who had distanced themselves, these pioneers studied how they might reach post-'60s generations with the gospel. Borrowing from the world of advertising and commerce, they resolved to do market studies. In short, they asked those of the disaffected generations why they didn't go to church. The answers have been widely reported in the press. Those queried replied that church was boring. They didn't like the music. The sermons seemed unrelated to their world, they said. They felt off-balance in church buildings, and among church people with their special stained-glass clothing and manners.

It's hard to say whether these various assessments reflect first-hand experience with churches, or whether they were drawn from cultural stereotypes such as that projected by the "Church Lady" on the *Saturday Night Live!* show. Were they, perhaps, based on young adults' memories of church, formed when they were children at home? Memories colored by the distaste of ten-year-olds or fifteen-year-olds for their parents' agendas? Were they based, possibly, on brief encounters with churches where they had formed no long-term or in-depth relationships? Were they shaded, perhaps, by the cultural alienation that the '60s and post-'60s generations felt in relation to their parents' generation? Were they colored by the perception that while their parents conformed religiously, they showed few signs at home of taking the faith seriously? Or were they possibly based on the fact that many churches, content to repeat old patterns without review, had in fact permitted themselves to fall into deadly routines? Is it possible that many churches simply found it too difficult or too threatening to weigh whether there was a need for change? Were the churches of the old Protestant establishment guilty of a cultural arrogance that presumed that it was people's duty to find them, rather than their duty to search for ways of relating to the unchurched? The answers are unclear—and probably a mixture of all the above—but the fact remains that a generation or two have perceived the churches as out of touch.

Meeting the Crisis

Those creative thinkers who first took notice of this decided to try to create a new kind of church—one that would have none of the negatives associated with traditional churches. From their pioneering efforts have come a variety of independent congregations, some of which have grown so large that they are called megachurches. These independent congregations have deliberately shaped themselves to reach the disaffected—popularly called seekers. They have certain characteristics in common.

First of all, churches formed to meet the needs of seekers have no ties to a denomination. Market studies showed that denominational labels do not attract the targeted generations, and in fact frequently turn them off. With no denominational connections, the independent congregation doesn't have to deal with the controversies and hard choices faced by congregations denominationally and ecumenically linked to a national or even worldwide church family. Every decision can be decided locally, by a relatively homogeneous congregation that has no need to account to distant kin whose situations may be vastly different.

The new independent congregations have erected buildings that do not look or feel like traditional churches. They invite people to come to worship dressed in casual clothes. The music intentionally does not resemble traditional church music, but reflects the instrumentation and the beat familiar from the popular culture.

It is not uncommon for there to be no readings from scripture—although scripture may be quoted in brief snippets. Sermons—not always called that—address current issues related to the stresses of daily life, marriage, child-raising, etc., which are likely to preoccupy the targeted generations.

Although there might be a vocal or instrumental ensemble or soloists (electronically enhanced, as at concerts), there are no choirs, no organs, no hymnals, certainly no pews, and very often, no Christian symbols. The place of assembly resembles a theater, or other commercial space where people have come to feel at ease.

Frequently, the seeker-oriented churches use high-tech electronic systems to project slides or videos, and employ sophisticated sound systems. Approaches to worship in these new congregations vary, of course, but in many cases those assembled remain a largely passive audience. They participate little, if at all, in the proceedings. It might be hard to say whether there is, in these assemblies, any remnant of the service of the Word—but certainly there is no Sacrament.

These remarkable efforts to reach the disaffected generations often experience phenomenal success. Credit for these new departures belongs, more often than not, to ministerial leadership from churches far more conservative than most mainline Protestant churches. Ironically, they have been successful in reaching many of those whose antipathy to traditional churches lies in disenchantment with tradition and authority. And yet they have succeeded, very often, in turning the thought and opinion of their constituents into surprisingly traditional channels: the husband's obligation to be spiritual leader in the home, a distinct division of roles between the genders, suspicion of public schools, an often uncritical nationalism, and sometimes even bloc voting for candidates favored by clerical leaders. Credit must be given to those with the imagination and creativity to have responded to the cultural crisis that so deeply affects the churches. They set a stunning example for the rest of us of how to color outside the lines—to move out to meet a new situation instead of being overwhelmed by it.

Does It Work?

When clergy in mainline denominations finally awakened to the realization that society has shifted around them, they began to give attention to the fact that it's urgent to rethink old patterns in view of a new cultural situation. Willow Creek Church and other seeker congregations began to draw the attention of traditional churches. These new churches offered models of a fresh approach in a time of bewilderment and uncertainty. However, it's fair to say that, in some cases, mainline ministers and lay leaders have panicked when they have finally realized that their congregations have been getting smaller and smaller, with no sign of a reversal of fortunes at hand. Sound analysis and thoughtful planning rarely emerge when there's a state of desperation.

For some in leadership positions, the equation is a simple one: mainline churches are shrinking; seeker churches are growing. If we want to grow, the prescription is to find out what the seeker churches are doing, and imitate it. Panic militates against a judicious caution. Those who plan worship may be particularly vulnerable to throwing caution to the winds because, in most mainline theological seminaries, there has been little effort to teach prospective ministers about the history and meaning of Christian worship. Many are unprepared, having little to go on other than past experience—not always good—or the stunningly successful seeker models. While there is much to admire in the creativity of those who have made it their mission to reach disaffected generations, it's not a sure thing that their methods can or should be adopted wholesale and indiscriminately.

The churches designed and created for seekers, first of all, begin at a different place than most existing congregations do. The seeker churches begin from scratch as a single-generational church. This gives them the advantage of designing absolutely everything—from architecture to decor to music to teaching—for their targeted constituency—unchurched young adults. Already, that separates them from any traditional congregations. The vast majority of existing congregations did not limit their initial appeal to one generational group. From their beginnings, they are likely to have included people of a variety of ages and family formations. Certainly any congregation that is more than twenty years old will have in its membership at least some retirees, some near the end of their working lives, and a number of empty-nesters, as well as parents of young children. There will be some widows and widowers, and some members who will bring to church with them elderly parents. The teaching, architecture, music, and program of these existing congregations will not have been designed with the interests of only one generation in mind. Younger and older share the same space and the same services of worship. So, the first question to any who are planning to introduce a seeker service on the Willow Creek model is, "Who do you expect to come to this service?"

If you are starting a new service on the seeker-service model, do you expect those who will attend it to come entirely from outside your congregation? Or do you expect that the worshiping core of this service will come from within the existing congregation? Second, is the seeker service intended to provide the complete worship diet for those who attend it? Or is it meant simply as an entry point that will lead people, eventually, into another sort of service?

The churches developed precisely for seekers use their Sunday assemblies to reach people turned off by the worship they have experienced in traditional churches. However, in many cases, the intention is that once the targeted constituencies make a Christian commitment, they will be led into another sort of service that occurs at a different time—usually during the week. The service offered on Sundays is today's equivalent of the old-time tent revival meeting. The intention behind those old-fashioned tent revivals was to reach people who didn't go to church. The goal was to win a commitment and to incorporate new converts into the ongoing life of an ordinary congregation. It was not intended—in most cases—that the worship of the tent revival be the standard worship diet of a Christian congregation. The tent revival was meant to be accessible to the curious and to provide an entry for those who might be unlikely to step inside a church building. A case can be made for a seeker service if it fulfills a similar function. However, if the seeker service is meant to substitute for the regular worship of the church, there is wisdom in thinking twice about that. Or, if those who attend such services see them as all they want or need in the way of worship, it will be wise to ponder the liabilities.

Why Can't the Seeker
Service Serve As the Chief Diet of Worship?

Christian worship is not passive. It's not enough simply to be present as a spectator or part of an audience, observing and listening to presentations made by a few for the pleasure or edification of the many. In fact, the Protestant Reformers objected in particular to the passivity of the congregation in the worship of the medieval church. Christian worship is active, and it requires the active participation of the assembly in one way or another.

Christian worship is rooted in scripture. It requires of us that we learn—or at least be attentive to—the stories and the language of scripture. Scripture must be read and preached in such a way as to provide an instrument by which Father, Son, and Holy Spirit may address God's people and become present to them. Scripture read and preached requires that, to some extent, we move into a world that is different from our own. Not that we must necessarily imagine ourselves in an ancient world, but nevertheless we must step out of our everyday presumptions into the larger world revealed in the gospel. Sermons (or "Christian presentations," as some call them) must be more than advice on how to reduce stress and solve problems.

Christian worship is sacramental. It looks for God in the water, symbols, and words of baptism; and in the bread and cup blessed and shared in the Lord's Supper. Christian worship is an exercise in losing oneself in order to find oneself as part of the body. It is a meeting of a people with that people's God—in Word and in Sacrament. To banish the sacramental from the ordinary worship diet of the church is to create a lopsided and diminished form of service that is inevitably crippled and out of balance.

Christian worship is the worship of a community. The Apostles' Creed speaks of the communion of saints. Saints are not super-good, ultra-holy people. Saints are all those who believe and are baptized—including those in our own generation, as well as generations past and generations to come. We are accountable to a community that has a story which began before we were born and will continue after we are gone. The worship that has distinguished that community from the very beginning is worship that combines synagogue service and meal—Word and Sacrament. We cannot discard our history. Each new generation experiences Word and Sacrament in continuity with every other.

So—wise and thoughtful planners of worship will necessarily think through the question of the role they expect a new seeker service to play within the total worship life of a congregation. Is there the serious prospect of drawing people who would ordinarily be classified as unchurched? Or is it likely to draw people who are already a part of the worshiping community, and who might better be encouraged to go deeper into the existing worship life of the congregation? Is there available in the congregation regular worship not intended merely as an entry point, but rather to provide nourishment to those who are consciously and intentionally Christian?

Planning Ahead—With Caution

Some established congregations provide an alternative service that they describe as contemporary. Use of that adjective requires that other services be described as traditional. These designations are unfortunate and even misleading. All worship that takes place in our own time is contemporary, whatever its style; and all worship that is intentionally Christian worship is, in some respects at least, traditional. The use of these labels may push worship leaders to be overzealous in trying to distinguish one service from the other. When we describe a service as traditional, many will wrongly hear that as hopelessly old-fashioned.

Does this mean that there is no room for variations in worship? Certainly not. Worship has always varied from time to time, and from place to place. High Mass at St. Patrick's Cathedral doesn't look or feel exactly the same as a communion service at a Baptist church of 150 members somewhere outside Joplin, Missouri. Even so, these two services may have more in common than seems likely at first sight. But there is a great deal of room for variation in worship rooted in Word and Sacrament.

Some who have thought carefully about how the church can relate to a new situation have used mission churches in other countries to clarify their thought. One hundred fifty years ago, Christian missionaries in India often built churches like the ones they knew back home in England or North America. They erected Gothic churches or New England-style colonial churches, or churches that would look quite natural on a public square in Savannah. Further, the missionaries (in Korea or Japan or the Belgian Congo) tended to introduce the same sort of music they were accustomed to back home in the Midwest or southern United States, or small towns in Scotland or England. Many of the churches that sprang from these missionary endeavors are still today singing the gospel songs popular in the days when the missionaries first left home. Does it make sense that Africans should have to accompany their hymns with organ music? In mission circles today, strategists are talking about indigenization and inculturation. What those fancy words mean is that when Christianity enters a new culture, it needs to make itself at home. In other words, although the faith does not change, the clothes it wears may. Doesn't it make more sense to build a church in India using Indian forms of architecture? To sing hymns in the Congo using African rhythms and instruments?

If it makes sense for the Christian faith to make itself at home in different cultures, doesn't it also make sense for it to make itself at home in different *North American* cultures? And, to the extent that different generations create and enjoy different cultures, might it not be possible that even something as sacred as Christian worship might look different in one generational culture than another? I think that the answer is Yes—with a caution. The caution might best be expressed by Dean Inge who warned that "he who weds the spirit of the age soon finds himself widowed." (Pardon the gender-exclusive language! The saying surely applies equally to both sexes.) Some churches that have tried to follow the recipe for creating services attractive to younger generations have discovered that styles change so much in five to ten years that their attempts to be up-to-date appear just as clumsy as an adult who tries to adopt adolescent jargon.

It's also important to bear in mind that the gospel does not call us to separation, but to reconciliation. Just as the distinctions between Jew and Gentile, or male and female, become secondary for those who are in Christ, so also do generational distinctions. It's a sad enough commentary on the American church that most congregations are mostly white, or mostly African-American, or mostly Hispanic, or mostly middle-class, or mostly blue-collar without willingly and knowingly creating another class of segregation by generation. The church is most able to represent God's intention for the world when the grand diversity of the human race is at least partly exhibited in the community assembled at worship. The purest worship is that which brings together old and young, adults and children, boomers and gen-xers and the generations that bracket them at either end.

Still another caution may be that the gospel ought never to be entirely at home in any culture. If gospel and culture fit together as easily as hand-in-glove, then the likelihood is that the gospel has capitulated to the values of the culture. Churches have become cheerleaders or mascots for cruel regimes and demonic causes. They have blessed superficial and sentimental substitutes for the biblical faith. There must always be some tension between gospel and culture. The trick is to tune that tension just right, so that gospel and church can play a transforming role in its host culture. The gospel doesn't carry with it a culture of its own. It must always find its place in the culture of the time and place. Nevertheless, it always questions the local culture and holds it accountable before the cross.

Viable Options

However, some things held sacred by traditionalists are not sacred at all. It's possible to have authentic Christian worship without an organ, without pews, hymnals, bulletins, or stained glass. It's possible to have authentic Christian worship without sitting quietly in rows, our backs to one another. Worshipers don't have to read in unison from a printed page. Music may incorporate all sorts of rhythms and all sorts of instruments, from flutes to drums to electronic keyboards. The tone of a service may be exuberant, as African-American Christians demonstrate frequently. And there is no reason why worship should categorically exclude visual art—including the electronic variety. Gutenberg's printing press introduced a new technology that had a significant impact on Christian worship. Microchip technology may have a place in our worship, too.

Many congregations, sensitive to cultural changes and desiring to reach out to new generations, have tried to make their existing worship seeker-friendly. In other words, they have tried to see their worship through the eyes of someone with no experience.

Why, for example, do we take it for granted that everyone knows the Lord's Prayer? Is there any reason it shouldn't be printed in the bulletin or projected overhead so as to make it accessible to one who's never heard it? Photocopy machines make it easy to include sung musical texts—even those as familiar as the Gloria Patri or the Doxology—without requiring that the newcomer look for them in the hymnal. Some congregations, hoping to be sensitive to seekers while recognizing a responsibility to their existing membership, have attempted to be broadly inclusive in their worship styles. These may incorporate music that is more easily accessible or more familiar in style to younger generations, while continuing to use older musical forms in the same service. Frequently, they also use other instruments along with the organ—keyboard, for example, and percussion instruments. Some congregations have offered services at unconventional times, like Saturday late afternoon or evening, to attract people who either work on Sunday mornings or, perhaps, have unpleasant associations with Sunday church. In some places, other rooms than the sanctuary better accommodate worshipers who want to see each other's faces, or to stand in a circle around a Communion Table, or otherwise move from set places during the service. One can make a case for adapting existing services or creating new ones with unreached persons specifically in mind. (In an established congregation, it's often easier to start a new service than to introduce radical changes in an existing one; however, for those for whom a single service is the only realistic option, variations on familiar patterns, introduced slowly and carefully, may be an answer.) Sensitivity to the stranger—whatever the form of a congregation's worship—is always important. And worship that appeals to younger generations will be relational and experiential—not merely passive or intellectual. It's at this point that the recovery of sacramental worship can make a substantial contribution.

What's Essential?

If so many variations are possible, what's really essential to Christian worship? I would argue that, for the churches of the

Protestant Reformation, it's first of all essential to recognize that we worship a BIG God! There's an old slogan—so old that the original is in Latin!—*Lex orandi, lex credendi*. It means, more or less, that the way we worship shapes the way we believe. If our worship is shallow, or if the worshiper takes center stage at God's expense, we run the risk of diminishing the God we're supposed to believe in. For example, if worship is based primarily on our various perceived needs, God may either get lost in the process, or be reduced to the status of a handy little helper. It's necessary to take care in the formation of worship that the materials we use don't diminish God. There are certain kinds of music that are very familiar to a generation of TV watchers—but they closely resemble the music of commercials, which easily set us to humming, but quickly become annoying. And, since we have grown suspicious of advertising, that sort of music may, in some deep corner of our minds, cause us to put up walls of resistance. Sacred texts require a music strong enough to bear them. A trivial music, or songs or hymns with trivial words, will make holy things seem trivial. Music must always serve worship rather than drive it or overwhelm it.

In shaping worship, the question must always be, "Are these materials worthy of a BIG God?" Or are we so set on making God accessible that we cut God down to a manageable size—the size of our helpful colleague or our therapist?

Either a very simple service or a very elaborate service is capable of bringing us before a BIG God. Styles, instruments, melodies, rhythms, colors, architecture, use of space, and movement may be adapted to a variety of cultures. But Christian worship will always be Trinitarian (what other God can we speak of with any authority?). Because it is Trinitarian, it will always be communal and relational—not merely passive. It will be something we enter into and do, rather than receive as an audience or as spectators. Worship that is identifiably Christian must be scriptural, oriented towards hope, serious about praying for and serving the world outside our doors, and confident that God is in charge. And it will always root itself in the two gifts that have distinguished it from the very beginning—synagogue service and meal—Word and Sacrament.